TRADITIONAL SAMPLERS

SARAH DON

While you my dear your needlework attend
Observe the counsel of a faithful friend
And strive an inward ornament to gain
Or all your needlework will prove in vain.

DAVID & CHARLES
Newton Abbot   London

To Betty, Jobo, Bewick, Nellie and Sasha

(frontispiece)
A Spanish sampler showing a large number of geometric border patterns worked mostly in satin stitch; other stitches used are hem, back, diagonal chevron, four-sided and outline stitches, with bullion knots. It is signed Gertrudes de Cpayso and dated 1729. The materials are silk on linen and the work measures 36 × 26½in (91.4 × 67cm) *(Victoria and Albert Museum, London)*

British Library Cataloguing in Publication Data

Don, Sarah
  Traditional samplers.
  1. Samplers
  I. Title
  746.44   NK9204

  ISBN 0-7153-8713-8

Typeset by ABM Typographics Limited, Hull
and printed in Great Britain
by Redwood Burn Limited, Trowbridge, Wilts
for David & Charles Publishers plc
Brunel House   Newton Abbot   Devon

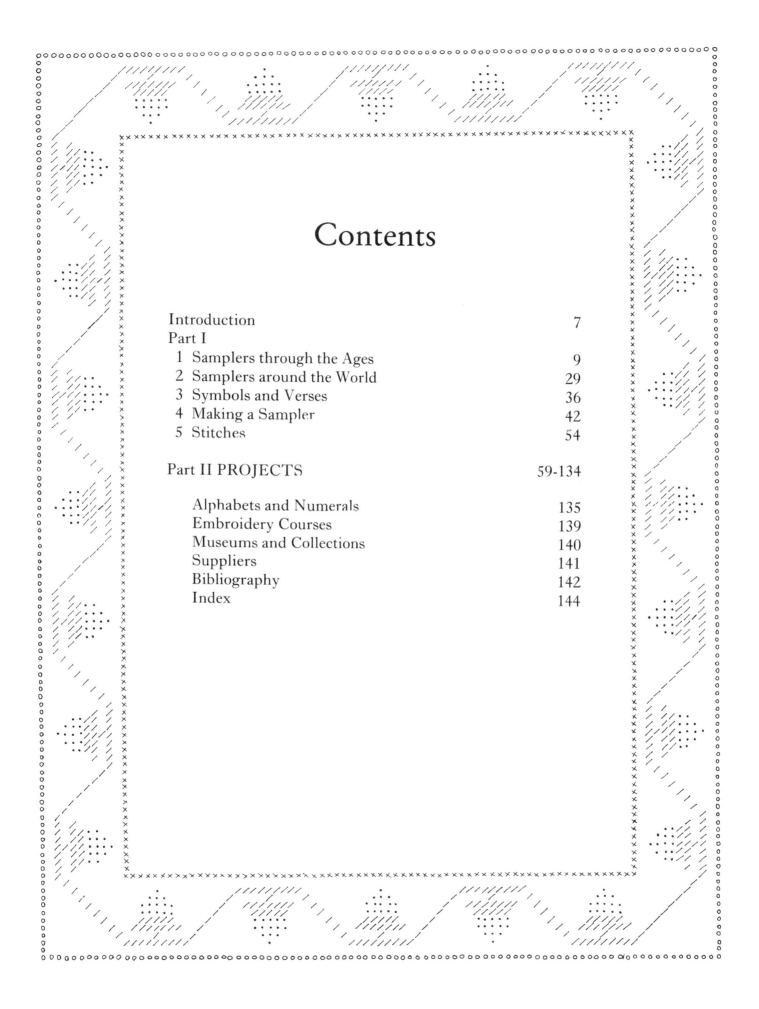

Contents

ABCDEFGHIKLMNOPQRSTVWXY IANE ROSTOCKI 1598
ALICE·LEE·WAS·BORNE·THE·23·OF·NOVEMBER·BE
ING·TWESDAY·IN·THE·AFTER·NOONE·1596

IVNO

Introduction

Like all traditional crafts, sampler-making has only been successful when it has served a purpose or fulfilled a need. Some of the most beautiful samplers are those made before the advent of printed patterns, when patterns and motifs were embroidered onto fabric to provide a useful record for future use. Later, samplers were used as practice pieces; on them the embroiderer would experiment with different stitches, colours and threads, and work out designs for other, more major, works. By the eighteenth century, samplers were the means by which young girls learnt the skills of needlework; later, in schools, they became useful exercises for teaching, for example, mathematical tables and geography. Poor children in schools and orphanages were taught only the most basic skills and worked row upon row of alphabets and numerals onto their samplers. It was hoped that these children would eventually obtain employment in service, having become proficient in the marking of linen, darning and mending.

When samplers were worked for their decorative value alone, standards deteriorated rapidly. The advent of the craze for Berlin woolwork during the Victorian era heralded the decline of the sampler, both throughout Europe and, later on, in America.

Sampler-making today is gaining in popularity and samplers are being made both by serious students of embroidery and by needlewomen who consider their craft a hobby. Sampler-making will survive so long as the finished works serve some real purpose, whether as practice pieces for beginners, notebooks for students or commemorative pieces depicting an historical occasion or a family tree.

This book has been written in the hope that it may promote and encourage the art of sampler-making, and prove a useful source of reference. There are traditional patterns and motifs from samplers over the last five centuries which have successfully survived many fashions and trends and, I believe, remain valid designs for working onto textiles today.

The complete samplers are intended for beginners and for those who may lack the confidence to design their own work. I am sure that after working one of the projects here, you will have gained sufficient skills and confidence to attempt working some of your own ideas. Try experimenting with colours, threads and fabrics. The materials and colours given with each project are intended as a rough guide and do not have to be followed slavishly. The same applies where there is text included in the work: use the text of your own choice — perhaps a favourite verse or a dedication.

I have tried to cover samplers from many different periods, including pieces from the Victorian era, whitework, blackwork, a number of alphabets, a multiplication table and a rebus sampler showing the story of Noah's Ark. The range of complexity of the samplers and of the skill required is also as wide as possible and I hope I have catered for all abilities.

I should like to encourage all embroiderers to explore the possibilities of further education through the various guilds and institutions that exist; a brief list of these is given, together with their addresses, at the end of the book. There is also a list of relevant publications in the bibliography; those that are possible sources of patterns and motifs are marked with an asterisk.

A very famous English sampler, worked by Jane Bostocke in 1598 to celebrate the birth of her daughter, Alice. A very large number of border patterns and all-over repeat patterns have been worked, together with a lion, a deer, a dog and a tiger standing over a daisy pattern border. Some of these patterns have been included in the project for the blackwork sampler. The threads used for the sampler are metal threads and silk on linen, with the inclusion of pearls and beads. The stitches used include back, satin, chain, ladder buttonhole, detached buttonhole, cross, arrowhead, interlacing, pattern couching, coral and two-sided Italian cross stitches with speckling, bullion and French knots. This sampler measures 17 × 15in (43 × 38cm) *(Victoria and Albert Museum, London)*

Note: When working with the charts and colour photographs the colours of the threads may not match exactly with the colours shown in the photographs, due to variations in printing and changes in dye lots for the threads. The latter can cause differences noticeable easily by eye.

1
Samplers through the Ages

Early Samplers

The word exampler or sampler is derived from the French *examplair*, meaning a kind of model or pattern to work by, copy or imitate. The Latin word *exemplum*, meaning a copy, pattern or model, was, by the sixteenth century, spelt *saumpler, sampler* or *exampler*.

The earliest surviving samplers are those worked in double running stitch and pattern darning; they were recovered from Egyptian burial grounds and are probably medieval. European embroideries were almost certainly influenced by the patterns on these works which had designs based on the ancient lozenge, S and X forms worked in running stitch.

As a result of the Renaissance movement, there was a strong revival of European interest in all forms of decoration in the late fifteenth and early sixteenth centuries. Many women took to the art of needlework to decorate not only personal attire, but also furnishings around the home. It was a most pleasurable pastime but a costly one; silk, gold and silver threads, beads and even tiny seed pearls were all expensive materials, so the craft was restricted to rich, often titled, ladies.

At this time there were no printed patterns available for needleworkers; patterns were passed from hand to hand, many slowly filtering through the Continent from the Middle East. This process was accelerated by the sudden increase in travel and foreign activity at this time.

The recording of patterns and motifs on fabric for future use was an essential task and resulted in the creation of the sampler. New patterns and stitches were avidly collected and exchanged among friends and were immediately added to the sampler before they could be forgotten. They were placed in a random or haphazard way over the cloth to fill every vacant space, hence the name random or spot sampler. These pieces were excellent practice grounds too, with the needleworker jotting down new stitches and experimenting with colours and threads, perhaps before proceeding to a more major work.

English sixteenth-century samplers were always worked on a linen ground with silk threads, although some examples also used gold and silver threads and seed pearls. The shape was narrow — 6-9in (15-23cm) wide and up to 24in (61cm) long, the length being determined by the loom width of the woven cloth.

The work on these samplers is so well executed that it is believed to be that of adult and expert needlewomen. Numerous geometric patterns were worked; excellent use was made of silk and metal threads; and many different stitches resulted in stunningly beautiful designs. Along with these patterns was worked a large range of spot motifs — a huge variety of flowers and animals from domestic animals such as dogs, horses, hares and swans to exotic creatures such as peacocks, lions and leopards. Any spaces occurring between these were filled with smaller creatures such as birds and insects, caterpillars, fish, snakes, frogs and butterflies. Some of the many stitches used were Hungarian, Florentine, tent, cross, long-armed cross, two-sided Italian cross, rice, running, double running, Algerian eye and buttonhole stitches.

Twenty different colours might be used on one piece of embroidery and these were tried out first on the worker's sampler. Popular colour schemes at the time were in different shades of blue, green, yellow, orange, brown and red, with an even larger number of shades being created by twisting together strands of two different colours. The resulting samplers would be highly treasured possessions, so much so that they were often bequeathed by will or mentioned in royal inventories.

The demand for printed patterns for needlework

An English sampler of the first half of the seventeenth century with numerous spot motifs and geometric patterns in a very large number of stitches including plaited braid, rococo, tent, back, crosslet, Algerian eye, interlacing, long-armed cross, Hungarian, Florentine, Roumanian, guilloche and chain stitches, with buttonhole wheels and laid and couched work. The threads used are silver, silver-gilt and silk on linen and the piece measures only 20½ × 12in (52 × 30.5cm). The patterns include diaper designs filled with acorns and floral motifs, knot patterns and repeating motifs. A number of small creatures have also been included — a frog, a caterpillar, duck and fish, together with various butterflies. This example illustrates the way in which these early samplers were used as notebooks and practice pieces *(Victoria and Albert Museum, London)*

was eventually exploited commercially and the first printed pattern book arrived in 1523, printed in Augsburg, Germany, by Johann Sibmacher. Similar books then appeared from French and Italian presses and finally in England from 1587. One pattern book, published in 1587 under the title *Singolari e Nuovi Disegni* and designed by Federico Vincioli, was to influence samplers in the sixteenth and seventeenth centuries. (The book has been reprinted as *Renaissance Patterns for Lace, Embroidery and Needlepoint.*) Italian work of the time showed a strong Islamic influence and was distinguished by its strongly geometric and elaborate floral borders. Pattern books were not commonly available and samplers continued to be made as reference sheets and practice pieces.

In England at this time, one of the most effective types of embroidery was blackwork. This technique used a single thread of black silk worked in double running stitch on a white or cream linen ground, and was to remain popular well into the seventeenth century. It was worked on clothes, chiefly cuffs and collars, in an extremely effective way. Double running stitch was particularly useful for this purpose as it had no wrong side, being worked twice along the design, first in one direction and then back again. Catherine of Aragon arrived in England from Spain in 1501 and the introduction of blackwork into Britain is popularly attributed to her, although examples had existed before her arrival. The patterns used for blackwork do have strong Moorish influences and geometric patterns worked in back stitch had been traditional in Spain for centuries. I am sure, however, that Catherine's arrival in England did promote the popularity of blackwork, and one of the names by which the running stitch became known was Spanish stitch. It was also given the name Holbein, because the painter of that name regularly had sitters wearing clothes decorated with blackwork embroidery.

Patterns originally printed for lacemaking during the Renaissance period showed linear designs which were eagerly and easily adapted for blackwork. With the increased circulation of engraved illustrations, designs such as those for formal gardens and knot gardens were also an inspiration. They were particularly suitable for blackwork, but also provided ideas for other types of embroidery; many beautiful pieces inspired by gardens and garden designs have been worked.

Few samplers from the sixteenth century have survived, and the signing and dating of samplers during this period was not common. The earliest dated surviving sampler was made by Jane Bostocke (p6). It was discovered as recently as 1960 and is one of the most famous samplers in the Victoria and Albert Museum in London. It was probably worked as a gift for Jane's daughter and she has included the inscription:

A sampler from the middle of the seventeenth century upon which have been worked a number of floral motifs and geometric patterns which I find particularly fascinating. These all-over repeating patterns are fairly simple and could easily be adapted for use today. The threads used are silver, silver-gilt and silk on linen, the stitches are eye, plaited braid, Florentine, Hungarian, cross, crosslet, long-armed cross, tent, Roumanian, rococo, gobelin, interlacing and drawn-fabric stitches. The sampler measures 20 × 8in (51 × 20cm) *(Victoria and Albert Museum, London)*

ALICE:LEE:WAS:BORNE:THE:23:OF:
NOVEMBER:BEING:TWESDAY:IN:
THE:AFTER:NOONE:1556.

The sampler is worked in red, brown, blue and white silks and includes black beads, seed pearls and metal threads, using back, satin, chain, two-sided Italian, cross, buttonhole and coral stitches and French knots. Some of the patterns (and the alphabet) on this sampler are used in the Blackwork Sampler (17).

During Elizabeth I's reign in England, trade with the East and the New World gave a terrific impetus to all the arts. The arrival of new materials and ideas from abroad began the exciting developments which led traditional English embroidery into the seventeenth century, now known as the golden age of sampler-making.

Seventeenth-century Samplers

In the seventeenth century, samplers were comparatively numerous and some of the most beautiful and

This distinctive Mexican sampler from the late eighteenth or nineteenth century contains a number of realistically worked motifs including birds, flowers, a butterfly or moth, a rather lovely rabbit and what appears to be a poodle carrying a basket of flowers. Silver-gilt thread and pure silk are worked on linen, with the inclusion of spangles. Long and short, satin and stem stitches with French knots are used and the sampler measures 12 × 15½in (30.5 × 39cm) *(Victoria and Albert Museum, London)*

imaginative pieces ever made come from the UK. At the beginning of this century, most were still being made as records and practice pieces for patterns, motifs and stitches. The designs and colour schemes were quite exquisite and the standards of stitchery and technique were very high.

Samplers produced in Germany at this time were either worked using a very simple floral border to surround a number of small geometric motifs placed at random, or included alphabets and border patterns as well as a number of motifs, again randomly placed.

The motifs included the instruments of the Passion, birds, animals, fruit trees and castles. The samplers were similar to those being made in England: long and narrow in shape and mostly worked in cross stitch in a number of colours.

Dutch samplers from this time were very like their German counterparts in the choice of subjects depicted and general layout, but they were distinguished by their shape — they were either square or wider than they were long.

It would seem that Spanish and Mexican samplers were being made in the sixteenth and seventeenth centuries, though very few have survived. Using brightly coloured silks of a number of different colours on white linen, they were given rather elaborate treatment. Satin stitch was predominantly used for the geometric motifs and patterns, with alphabets and verses appearing rarely. Spanish samplers were square or rectangular and frequently signed and dated. Mexican samplers were usually rectangular with motifs such as animals and birds placed at random.

French samplers were square or broader than they were long and were worked almost entirely in cross stitch. Italian samplers were also wider than they were long, but included the use of other stitches such as feather, double running, satin and chain stitches.

In England, during Charles I's reign, there was a tremendous increase in the wealth of society; much of this money was spent on elegant refinements and large quantities of household linens and furnishings. Ladies found the skill of needlework to be a highly desirable asset and used embroidery to decorate these furnishings and items of attire.

The number of pattern books in circulation increased. These included the famous *A schole-house for the needle,* by Richard Shorleyker, published in 1624. The following lines are from the poem 'The Needle's Excellency' by John Taylor. This was later also the title for a book, the twelfth edition of which was published in London in 1632; it consisted of needlework patterns originally published in Germany in 1597 under the title *Schön Neues Modelbuch,* by Johann Sibmacher.

Here Practice and Invention may be free,
And as a Squirrell skips from tree to tree,
So maids may (from their Mistresses, or their Mother)
Learne to leave one worke, and to learne an other,
For here they may make choyce of which is which,
And skip from worke to worke, from stitch to stitch,
Until, in time, delightfull practice shall
(with profit) make them perfect in them all.

In the early part of the century, samplers continued to be worked by adult needlewomen and were still in the form of the spot or random samplers of the sixteenth century, recognisable by their long and narrow shape. These samplers were particularly colourful and imaginative. Animals, both real and mythological, birds and flowers were worked in very fine tent stitch with a high degree of shading. The designs of this period strongly reflect the current fashions of the time. A wide range of fauna and flowers appears, with the Tudor rose being the favourite. Roses were the national emblems of the Tudor kings and appear on samplers as red and white flowers, usually in full face rather than in bud; both single and double varieties were depicted. Carnations, pansies, tulips, lions and stags appear regularly, along with snails, caterpillars, butterflies and fish. Favourite fruits were pineapples, figs, grapes and strawberries. Animals were to become increasingly popular towards the latter half of the century. The earliest recorded human figures on a sampler appear on a piece dated 1630. Samplers of this time were rarely signed in full and only a few included the initials of the needleworker.

The band sampler was popular in this century and consisted of tightly packed rows of border patterns with hardly a space left unworked and using a wide variety of stitches. Most of the linen used for these samplers was imported and was still very costly; hence the obvious need to economise with fabric. The threads used were silk, gold and silver, with beads, seed pearls and sequins incorporated into the designs.

The bands of patterning had both geometrical and floral designs and, as with the spot samplers, used roses, carnations and strawberries in repeating border patterns. Another popular motif worked into border patterns was the acorn. This was shown both on its own and with the oak leaf; although it appears on many samplers from this century, it was to disappear completely by the beginning of the eighteenth century.

Patterns outlined with running stitch were still popular but, over the years, workers began to fill them in with coloured silks and metal threads, using a number of different stitches.

Assisi work, which originated in northern Italy, was often included on these samplers for a few rows, or in deep borders at the edges of linens. Popular motifs worked and repeated across borders were birds, rosettes, stars, hearts and heraldic animals. They were sewn using a number of different stitches including cross stitch, tent, single-faggot and plaited-braid. Older pieces used outlines of back stitch, buttonhole or whipping stitch.

'Boxers' were representations of the human form and were usually worked in back stitch or running stitch; later on they were filled in with coloured silks, usually in satin stitch. These figures are often depicted carrying what could be a heart shape, an acorn or perhaps a flower. In modern days they have been given the name 'boxers' because of their stance. One

An English band sampler of the mid-seventeenth century which has a number of motifs worked in double running stitch and wide floral bands of patterning. The motifs include a lion and a unicorn; charts for the strawberry plant and a number of the smaller floral motifs are given in the blackwork project on page 116. The materials used for the band sampler are silk on linen, in double running, stem, Montenegrin, cross, Algerian eye, outline and detached filling stitches. The sampler measures 18 × 7½in (45.5 × 19cm) *(Victoria and Albert Museum, London)*

explanation for their significance is that they are lovers exchanging gifts. A large flowering plant appearing between the figures is said to have originated as a female figure holding a gift (a sprig of foliage), which, through many translations and repeated copying, has been modified to the shape and form of a bush. Boxers have also been referred to as Renaissance cupids or as early versions of Adam and Eve.

Bands of more complicated whitework and open-work would often appear at the bottom of these samplers. Perhaps this kind of work was left to last, by which time the worker might have gained enough skill and expertise to execute the techniques proficiently.

Whitework is the name given to all types of embroidery on white linen worked with white thread, and the simplest forms are designs of block satin stitch, double running stitch and detached buttonhole bars. Cut and drawn work is more difficult. Geometric and floral designs are worked on a framework of threads which is first prepared by drawing out and cutting threads from a piece of linen and replacing them with diagonal threads. More complicated pieces included designs which depicted the human figure; Adam and Eve and mermaids were popular subjects.

The fashion for whitework was probably stimulated by the craze for lace which seemed to decorate every item of attire at this time. Whitework was a way of achieving a similar effect more quickly and was used for modest decoration on edges and hems. Denmark was the home of some rather beautiful pieces of whitework, as too was Sweden. During the period when only the nobility were permitted to wear lace, ordinary Danish women used whitework to decorate items of clothing.

Samplers worked solely in cutwork are in a much smaller group. One such piece which can be seen in the London Museum shows the arms of Queen Elizabeth I, which suggests that this type of work was current at the beginning of this century. The earliest signed and dated cutwork sampler was worked in 1634.

In England, during the early years of the reign of Charles I, the art of needlework became a well-established part of the school curriculum, with samplers being used to familiarise young children with the many different embroidery and lacework techniques.

By the mid-seventeenth century, alphabets were included in samplers, along with signatures at the bottom of the work. The neat rows of patterning and the inclusion of these alphabets were an indication that sampler-making was becoming more and more significant as a school exercise for children.

As printed patterns for needlework and designs printed on embroidery canvas became more readily available, the use of the sampler as a record was virtually over; but children's samplers were still meant

An Italian whitework sampler of the mid-seventeenth century which is signed Gvllia Piccolomini. A number of intricate and rather lovely geometric patterns have been worked in cut and drawn-thread work, using linen on linen. A female figure has been included in the bottom left-hand corner. Cut and drawn-thread work samplers were also being worked at this time in England, with the patterns tending more towards those based on floral designs. This sampler measures 32 × 18in (81 × 46cm) *(Victoria and Albert Museum, London)*

---

as practice pieces for the different stitches and as notebooks of patterns for future use. Alphabets were needed for marking linen, and spot motifs would be used for smaller items such as purses and pincushions. Some lovely examples of whitework and cutwork were being worked by children and still had practical uses up to the middle of the seventeenth century. By this time, the borders worked on samplers had become over-fussy and large and would have been far too elaborate to work on household linen.

The children's work was of a very high standard and used remarkably varied techniques. The samplers were a credit to the thoroughness of the teachers' instruction and the teacher's name was often included in the finished piece.

From about 1650 onwards, short, pious, moral and religious inscriptions were often added. Utility was now obviously a secondary consideration and samplers had become purely beginners' exercises in fine needlework. The teaching of needlework in schools was encouraged by the Protestant ethic which considered it an excellent way of discouraging idleness in young girls aged between eight and eleven years. The eighteenth-century dictionary definition by Samuel Johnson of the word 'sampler' was 'a piece worked by young girls for improvement'. This was the mood in which sampler-making entered the eighteenth century.

Eighteenth-century Samplers

Embroidery in general at this time continued to flourish, being strongly influenced by the many exotic textiles imported from India, China and Persia. Unfortunately, however, the standard of sampler-making was to deteriorate rapidly from now on, with samplers being worked by children as young as five years. It is not really surprising that the new-found embroidery techniques and fashions being worked by adult needlewomen did not appear on these children's samplers. The children used far fewer stitches, and much brighter colours.

In Germany during the eighteenth century, another type of sampler was being worked using just one or

14

two colours. Black thread was worked on a cream ground using cross stitch, or red was used on a white ground with a variety of stitches, including satin, hem and eyelet stitches.

The shape of samplers was also changing. In England they were shorter and wider, taking on the proportions of a picture. Samplers had lost their need for utility and could now be classed as needlework pictures. They were intended to be ornamental and the finished work would be displayed in the home by proud parents as a record of their child's achievement at school.

English samplers consisted of stylised borders surrounding rows of alphabets and numerals, a lengthy piece of text or a short verse or inscription. Spaces were filled with symmetrically placed motifs, birds, small animals, flowers and trees. There were trees in every shape and size, with the conical tree the most popular. These motifs were often worked in pairs and were sparsely arranged around the sampler; the need to economise with fabric had apparently disappeared. The choice and arrangement of subject matter was very carefully thought out, in order to make a successful, well-ordered and balanced picture. Samplers of this century and the next were in complete contrast to the random spot and band samplers of earlier centuries which owed much of their beauty to the fact that their working was an essential art.

Nearly all samplers were now made by schoolchildren but the importance of needlework in schools had become secondary; the samplers were merely vehicles for instruction, primarily of religious and moral teachings and also for lessons on geography, English and mathematics. The most popular needlework exercises were almanacs, mathematical tables and maps, as well as the usual numbers and letters. The art of darning was learnt by children and darned samplers were popular in Germany, Holland and England. They were worked on rather fine material, such as muslin, using subtle colours, and counted-thread work.

Today these samplers give us a fascinating insight into the social history of the time. Although no longer works of art, they are still achievements in their own right, to be wondered at and admired. They possess a very special kind of charm, especially when we realise that children of such tender age endured the long and tedious task of stitching row upon row of alphabets, hymns and lengthy passages of religious and moralistic text (including the Lord's Prayer, the Ten Commandments and the Apostles' Creed).

In the latter half of this century, these inscriptions were generally replaced by shorter verses, though in the same tone. Those most commonly used were from the writings of Philip Doddridge, John Wesley and Dr Isaac Watts, whose book of *Divine and Moral Songs for Children* was addressed to 'all that are concerned in the education of children . . . whatever may conduce to give the minds of children a relish for virtue and religion. . . .' One of Dr Watts's verses which appeared on a sampler read:

Virtue's the chiefest beauty of the mind
The greatest ornament of mankind
Virtue's our safeguard and our guiding star
That stirs up reason when senses err.

The mortality rate of children at this time was very high and the religious population seemed to be preoccupied, almost obsessed, with the subject of death. The generally pessimistic and gloomy outlook on life was reflected in the verses used:

Our life is never at a stand
'Tis like a fading flower
Death is always near at hand
Comes nearer every hour.

Another verse on the same subject worked on a sampler was even shorter and more to the point:

When I am dead and worms me eat
Here you shall see my name complete.

The materials used at this time varied. Linen was still popular and in the first half of this century a fine woollen canvas called tammy cloth was much in vogue. This was susceptible to moths and did not remain popular for long. Needless to say, few pieces worked on this cloth have survived. Cotton was used occasionally at the end of this century, and satin was regularly used for map samplers. Satin could be bought with the map's outline already printed or hand-drawn onto it. Maps were also worked on fine silk gauze or tiffany, a fine muslin-like material.

The threads popularly used were still silk and linen, and later in the century, wool and cotton. Metallic threads were now very rarely used. Chenille was occasionally worked on map samplers; black silk and human hair added an air of sentimentality on mourning samplers. One such sampler bore the following inscription:

Heavenly Love
Christ's Arms Do Still Stand Open To Receive
All Weary Prodigals That Sin Do Leave
For Them He Left His Father's Blest Abode
Made Son Of Man To Make Man Son Of God
To Cure Their Wounds He Lives Elixir Bled
And Died A Death To Rise Them From The Dead.

This Work Was Done With The Hair of Mr Thomas Vickery
By Elizabeth, His Daughter, 1782.

In the middle of the eighteenth century, a relatively small number of stitches were being used, including cross stitch, Algerian eye, double running stitch and four-sided stitch; by the end of the century, cross stitch became the sole survivor of what was once an enormous repertoire of stitches used on samplers — it is often described as the sampler stitch.

The obsession with learning and stitching the alphabet which had begun in the seventeenth century, continued right through the eighteenth century, and finally receded in the early part of the nineteenth century. The simplicity and legibility of the letters were most important, and they were usually worked in cross stitch and Algerian eye. Very occasionally, elaborate initial letters appeared, worked in various stitches.

Many samplers showed the old alphabet, from which J and U were omitted, with I and V being used in their place. Q was often the same as P, but reversed. Z was often omitted altogether as a letter not much in use. Alphabets were usually laid out in rows, being worked across the sampler and divided by lines of border patterns varying in design, size and complexity.

Letters were occasionally worked in pairs — AA, BB, CC etc — using different stitches for the first and second letters. The capital and lower-case letters were also worked in pairs — Aa, Bb, etc. In most samplers, though, the capitals were worked first, with the lower-case letters being set out underneath. Spaces at the ends of rows were often filled in with small patterns or motifs — hearts, crowns and so on. If the sewer was feeling lazy, letters were missed out altogether, especially if the last few letters of the alphabet did not fit into the final line.

In Germany, alphabets were given extremely elaborate treatment using several colours and a number of different stitches. The same is true of samplers from Holland and Denmark, though to a lesser extent. Crowns and coronets, which often appeared on Dutch and German samplers, also featured on English pieces, because they were used in the linen-marking process. Each rank of nobility was denoted by its own distinctive coronet which would have been embroidered onto the linen above the owner's initials and the date on which the linen was acquired. Hearts, which were worked onto Central European samplers, did not often appear on English ones, although little flying cupids were quite popular.

English samplers with complex bands of patterning, including those with figures of boxers, did not die out until after the middle of this century along with any cut and drawn whitework. Very simple patterns worked in cross stitch appeared in the rows between alphabets; the older band patterns had become much simplified and were used as borders around the whole sampler. Printed cottons from India had influenced some of these patterns, which were now freer, more flowing and worked in brighter colours. Floral patterns were worked with more curving lines as opposed to the rather angular and geometric band-sampler patterns. The choice of patterns was probably determined by the teacher, as were the verses used, with a number of favourites appearing time and time again. Popular border patterns which appeared regularly such as the strawberry, rosebud and carnation designs, showed little variation or distortion over the years.

Some of the most charming samplers from England at this time were those made by the few very young children who were allowed to work their own ideas. They showed great imagination and originality, some working their own homes and members of their families, though they were rarely identified as such. Many samplers were worked in honour and gratitude to parents, thanking them for their care and guidance or for the child's education. The following two verses are typical of those which would be worked:

Dear mother I am young and cannot show
Such work as I unto your goodness owe
Be pleased to smile on this my small endeavour
I'll strive to learn and be obedient forever.

Oh smile on those whose liberal care
Provides for our instruction here;
And let our conduct ever prove
We're grateful for their generous love.

Houses and landscaped rural scenes, found on European samplers from earlier times, were increasingly occupying the lower halves of English samplers and would include shepherds and shepherdesses, dovecotes and windmills, animals, urns and vases. Forts and ships appeared sometimes, but were featured more on Dutch samplers. The people depicted on the rigging of these sailing ships are thought to represent members of the embroiderer's own family.

Other European samplers of the eighteenth century consisted mainly of a number of different motifs placed at random around the cloth and the subjects depicted might include the emblems of the Passion, flowers, trees and furniture. French samplers sometimes had a verse contained by a shield or cartouche. The subjects typical of Dutch and German samplers were dogs, deer and trees as well as many religious scenes. These included the return of the spies from Canaan, and Adam and Eve. Adam and Eve also became quite common on English samplers by the latter half of this century. They were usually shown beneath the Tree of Knowledge laden with apples and often with the serpent, itself a popular motif. The snake could be seen as a symbol either of evil, or of the Resurrection (because it shed its skin to emerge anew). Sometimes Adam and Eve would appear naked, and sometimes fully clothed. This verse is typical of the kind which would accompany these figures:

This charming little sampler of the mid-eighteenth century is signed Hannah Haynes and has cutwork with hollie point insertions. The cutwork is surrounded by a border of large flowers which are worked in satin, cross, rococo and back stitches with French knots. The background to this floral border has used satin stitch in a rather interesting way and there is a fascinating textural quality to the whole piece. The materials are silk and linen on linen and the sampler measures 8 × 8in (20 × 20cm) *(Victoria and Albert Museum, London)*

Adam and Eve whilst innocent
In paradise were placed
But soon the serpent by his wiles
The happy pair disgraced.

This following verse was a rather more compassionate one:

Adam alone in paradise did grieve
And thought Eden a desert without Eve
Until God, pitying his lonesome state
Crown'd all his wishes with a lovely mate
Then why should men think mean or slight her
That could not live in paradise without her.

Rebus samplers are those where words in a piece of text are replaced by a picture; they are quite rare. The story of Noah's ark lent itself well to this treatment: the words 'dove', 'ark' etc would be replaced by a pictorial rendering of a dove and an ark.

More popular were acrostic samplers where the first letter of the first word on each line, read vertically, spelt out a short message or the name of a person. The favourite acrostic was that of Christ, but quite often they were worked as memorial samplers.

Other favourite classroom exercises were almanacs, multiplication tables and tables for pounds, shillings and pence — though they could not always be relied upon to be correct. These were usually worked in cross stitch, perhaps with a pictorial scene below and with a patterned border around the whole.

From about 1770, map samplers became very popular and were worked in large numbers. The most common maps were those showing England and Wales, with just a part of Scotland and Ireland. Some, of particular interest, show local areas, and others a single county. Some map samplers covered two whole hemispheres — the Old and the New Worlds. France, Spain and Ireland were among the single countries worked. In America, children produced three dimensional globes of the world rather than maps. These map samplers were considered an excellent way of teaching geography to the children and although most were horribly inaccurate, because the children copied and drew the outlines themselves, their making was a reflection of the growing public interest in foreign travel and affairs.

Sometimes countries were outlined with chenille thread, and the lettering was usually worked in cross stitch or Algerian eye. The maps were worked on fine linen, silk gauze or taffeta and were often oval in shape, surrounded by a garland and bows or flowers. On maps of Britain, a wreath or scroll containing the maker's name and the date on which the piece was completed was placed in the North Sea. Most included the points of the compass and, very occasionally, a scale or lines of latitude.

Nineteenth-century Samplers

In England, rigid standards of morality and decency were to dominate in the reign of Queen Victoria and the majority of the population were very poor. There was a high demand for child labour and most young children of the poorer classes managed to earn a little extra money working down the coal mines and in the fields.

Before the invention of the sewing machine, in the first half of this century, many women and children worked with their needles in poverty and hunger, both in urban slums and in country villages:

Work, work, work
Seam and gusset and band,
Band and gusset, and seam,
Till over the buttons I fall asleep
And sew them on in a dream.

Thomas Hood: 'The Song of the Shirt'

Children as young as four years old spent all day in the tiny cramped rooms of the lace schools. They wound bobbins and helped their elders to sew lace; although conditions must have been terribly hard, this work was probably preferred to labouring in the coal mines.

Education at this time was sorely neglected, and until the introduction of state schools later in the century, the only form of education for poor children came from Sunday schools, charity schools and orphanages. Children who did attend these schools were not taught reading and writing; apart from moral instruction and Bible reading, they were taught only spinning, knitting and sewing. Girls who learnt to sew and darn then had the chance to find work in service with a family and although it was poorly paid work, it must have seemed much more comfortable than working in one of the factories and mills that were the backbone of the Victorian economy.

Most clothes at this time were made, altered and repaired at home and the obsession with marking every single item of clothing and household linen continued. There was plenty of sewing for the ladies' maid whilst the lady of the house busied herself with the management of her servants, good works, religion and childbearing. Ladies of the Victorian era spent most of their leisure time in the genteel art of embellishing and decorating every sort of household furnishing with needlework.

Charity samplers were developed to supply the children with the skills required for their future occupation. They were very plain and densely packed with hardly an inch left unworked, and the standard of work was generally very high. They were worked either on linen or a coarse-mesh canvas and the thread was usually wool, occasionally silk. More often than not they were in a single colour, either red or black — a characteristic of some earlier German samplers.

This sampler was worked by M. A. Tipper and includes the following inscription:

M A Tipper
New Orphan House
North Wing
Ashley Down
Bristol
1868.
(The 6 was later changed to 0, to make the sampler seem earlier)

M. A. Tipper was born on 16 September 1852 and was admitted to the orphanage in 1863, aged eleven years. This piece shows the purely functional purpose of samplers, to teach children the basic skills of sewing alphabets and numerals for marking linen. Nevertheless, this sampler must have been quite a feat, taking many hours to complete. The alphabets, numerals and border patterns are densely worked, showing strict economy of space and fabric *(Fitzwilliam Museum, Cambridge)*

This cushion was one of three samplers which are thought to have been worked in 1879 by Annie Parker, a prisoner at the Clerkenwell House of Correction. Annie (who served over 400 separate sentences for drunkenness) worked this sampler in human hair, presumably the only material to hand. The cushion has been worked using cross stitch and is decorated with a crocheted cotton-lace edging *(Black Museum, New Scotland Yard, London, by permission of the Commissioner of the Metropolitan Police)*

The stitches that the children were required to master included: back, buttonhole, chain, darning, herringbone, marking, basting, overcast and oellit stitches. As well as the usual rows of alphabets (up to twenty different versions might be worked on one sampler), and bands of simple patterning, the now statutory religious or moralistic text was worked, sometimes with a small Bible or crucifix in the centre. The upright alphabet was the most common; the sloping version also appeared and was used for marking fine linen. Each sampler was marked with both the name and address of the worker, and the date on which it was completed, along with a number which is thought to have been the child's identification number at the school or orphanage.

Schools often took in plain work, usually darning or repairing worn linen. The profits were to help fund the schools, but the children were probably considered cheap labour. Hannah More, who established the Mendip schools in the late eighteenth century, said: 'My plan of instruction is extremely simple and limited. They learn on weekdays such coarse works as may fit them for servants. I allow of no writing for the poor. . . .' Hannah even composed a series of moral tales and verses specially for the children.

The three Brontë sisters all produced samplers that were typical of this time and convey well the atmosphere of the times. The sisters were ten, eleven and thirteen years old and the samplers were sewn around the year 1830. They show a total lack of ornament and consist of lengthy pieces of religious text surrounded by very simple borders, worked in dark green silk on a rough textured canvas.

Later on in this century state schools were introduced and they too limited their curriculum to religion, good moral precepts and needlework. The children learnt only plain sewing, not fancy embroid-

ery techniques. This work included different kinds of seams, making buttonholes, darning and inserting cuffs and collars. School manuals produced during this century stressed the importance of women learning needlework so that they could obtain work in service. The following words appeared in the preface to *Plain Needlework in all its branches,* published in 1849 for use in the National Industrial School of the Holy Trinity, at Finchley, London.

> [The necessity for women to have] a practical acquaintance with needlework. . . . As regards plain needlework especially, this is more particularly the case with reference to females in humble life, whether with a view to domestic neatness and economy, or to profitable occupation in a pecuniary light.

In America, this acquaintance with needlework was also considered a most important part of a young girl's upbringing and was taught in schools across the country. American sampler-making developed rapidly and is discussed separately later in the book.

Apart from the very plain samplers, there were also those which did include motifs. These motifs, though, had become stereotyped and over-simplified and were arranged around the sampler in such a way that perfect symmetry was the paramount consideration. Animals, birds, flowers and trees were all perfectly balanced and often placed in pairs. The number of motifs in use was far fewer than in the eighteenth century and there was much less variety. Where houses and gardens were worked, they were very simply treated and all were worked in bold and rather garish colours.

The following quotation comes from a work by Sophia F. Caulfeild and Blanche C. Saward, under the heading 'To Make A Sampler':

> Take some Mosaic Canvas, of the finest make, and woven so that each thread is at equal distance apart. Cut this 18 inches wide and 20 inches long, and measure off a border all round of 4 inches. For the border, half an inch from the edge, draw out threads in a pattern to the depth

(cont on p24)

The top sampler was made by Emily Jane Brontë in March 1829 when she was eleven years old. The large amount of religious text which is surrounded by a Greek-key border must have been very boring to work and is typical of samplers from this time. It is worked with green-black silk on canvas and is similar to those worked by Emily's sisters *(Brontë Society, Brontë Parsonage, Haworth, West Yorkshire)*

Anne Brontë's sampler, dated Nov 28 1828. There are a few very simple border patterns and two alphabets with short pieces of religious text worked on rough canvas. It is a rather sombre piece, reflective of the sad times in the three sisters' lives. Charlotte Brontë's sampler is almost identical to this one of Anne's *(Brontë Society, Brontë Parsonage, Haworth, West Yorkshire)*

KNOW THYSELF ALL WISDOM CENTRES THERE.

PENCE				SHILLINGS		
d		s	d	s		£ s
12 are		1	0	20 are		1 0
20		1	8	30		1 10
24		2	0	40		2 0
30		2	6	50		2 10
36		3	0	60		3 0
40		3	4	70		3 10
48		4	0	80		4 0
50		4	2	90		4 10
60		5	0	100		5 0
70		5	10	110		5 10
72		6	0	120		6 0
80		6	8	130		6 10
84		7	0	140		7 0
90		7	6	150		7 10
96		8	0	160		8 0

Lifes but a span mans longest years
Are nothing Lord to thee
When fix'd in glory he appears
What splendid vanity

Worked with Miss E Geoghegan.

E Sherwin.
Aged 11 years.
1835

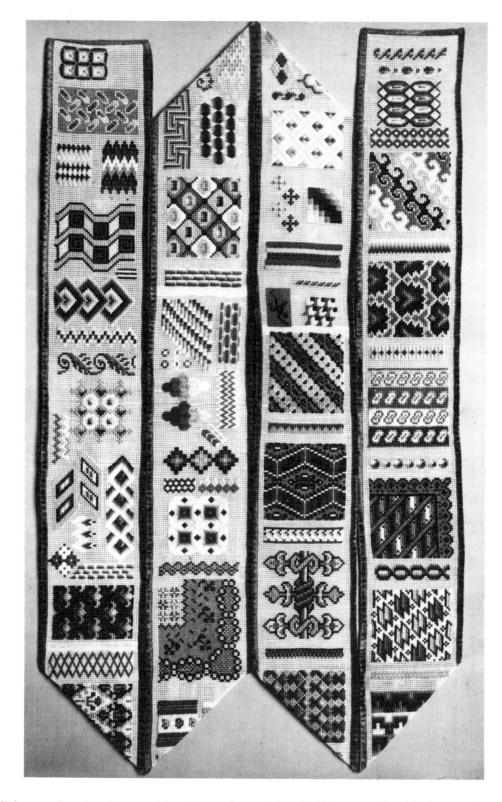

(opposite) English sampler showing a table of pounds, shillings and pence worked in 1835 by E. Sherwin, aged eleven (with the help of Miss E. Geoghegan). It uses eyelet and cross stitches, and a typical Greek-key border *(Brooklyn Museum, New York)*

(above) This type of mid-nineteenth century woolwork sampler was usually worked by professionals for display. The materials are silver thread, wool and silk on linen, and beads. Cross, Hungarian, satin, Florentine and brick stitches are used, with laid and couched work. It is 4in (10cm) by 10ft 1¼in (3m 3cm). The mainly geometric border and repeating patterns make good creative use of the different stitches *(Victorian and Albert Museum, London)*

of half an inch, and work over these with coloured silk; then work a conventional scroll pattern, in shades of several colours, and in tent stitch, to fill up the remaining 3 inches of the border. Divide the centre of the sampler into three sections. In the top section work a figure design. [In the old samplers this was generally a sacred subject, such as Adam and Eve before the Tree of Knowledge.] In the centre section work an alphabet in capital letters, and in the bottom an appropriate verse, the name of the worker, and the date.

All the decorative arts, including embroidery, deteriorated rapidly in this century, and became over-elaborate. From the 1830s onwards, embroidery was taken over by a passion for Berlin woolwork, a craze which spread through both Europe and America. The technique employed wool in rather bright and garish colours worked on double canvas in a wide variety of different geometric and floral patterns and using a large number of stitches.

Berlin wools, or zephyr yarns, were spun at Gotha in Germany and then dyed in Berlin. The patterns for this work also came from Berlin and the first printed patterns on graph paper were published in 1804–5 by a man named Philipson. These were imported to England in large numbers and by 1840, over 14,000 designs had been produced.

During the first half of the nineteenth century, great improvements had been made in the science of dyeing and after an English chemist called Henry Perkins had accidentally discovered a new dye which was to be called mauve, great use was made of new and exciting colours such as magenta and violet. The new Berlin wools were much softer than the previous hard, twisted worsted yarns and the colours were a great deal faster. The huge variety of different colours which was now available meant that a high degree of shading could be achieved, thereby giving more realistic renderings of the subjects being worked. Complete scenes were highly three-dimensional and the technique was rather like painting by numbers — indeed favourite paintings were often copied in great detail. Other threads such as silk and gold, and occasionally beads, were incorporated into the designs, so highlighting particular areas.

In England, the subjects most commonly worked were whole scenes or vignettes of domestic pets, and portraits of the royal family; Queen Victoria's King Charles spaniel, Dash, was a very popular subject. Floral and geometric motifs and patterns were also very popular and were used to furnish all sorts of household items including footstools, curtain ties, firescreens, cushions and even bell pulls.

By the end of the nineteenth century, children's samplers showed obvious influences from this craze for Berlin woolwork and included subjects similar to those currently being worked in wool by adult needle-women. Floral bouquets, landscaped scenes and family pets were all being worked, with rather crude attempts at the realistic shading which was characteristic of Berlin woolwork.

A very wide variety of canvas stitches was being employed, including Hungarian, Florentine, brick, a number of different cross stitches, Leviathan stitch and perspective stitch. There were many types of canvas available at this time. Berlin canvas was very fine, needed no grounding, and was available in black, white and pearl white, the last being the most expensive type. Penelope was a canvas which had groups of four threads (usually canvas for Berlin work had threads in pairs). German canvas was the least expensive and every tenth thread was yellow in order to make counting easier.

There is a group of Berlin woolwork samplers which were made at this time. These are long strips of canvas with blocks of floral and geometric patterns, often with simple border patterns appearing in between each. These were worked using many of the stitches popular at the time and are similar to the seventeenth-century band samplers. For a short time at least, samplers had regained their original purpose: it is believed that these Berlin woolwork samplers were intended as some kind of reference sheet, either for the needleworker's own use, or for resale in needlework shops for the amateur to copy.

Slowly, Berlin woolwork fell from favour and came under particular criticism from the Church and its architects who were taking an interest in embroidery; the work was considered purely an exercise in copying skills. In England, at the time of the Arts and Crafts Movement, William Morris and others were attempting to bring about a revival in the art of embroidery, but with little effect. These were days when machines were producing remarkable results in the field of textiles. Isaac Singer had produced the first successful sewing machine, and the first embroidery machine, which was invented in 1828, had been developed to produce rather sophisticated effects. Needlewomen were no longer attempting to create major works and did not see the need to learn the art of stitchery. Now this need had disappeared, the skills used for working fine embroidery were sorely neglected.

Happily, the art of embroidery is today experiencing a strong revival, with large numbers of embroiderers working in both traditional and contemporary styles. Samplers survive as beginners' pieces and as experimental grounds for more expert workers.

(*opposite*) Celebration of a Child's Birthday (p60)
(*overleaf, left*) Multicoloured Alphabets in Wool (p62); Spaniel (p64); (*right*) Adam and Eve (p66); Red and Green Alphabets (p68); Red Alphabets (p71)

Oliver Don Born 16 Jan. 1981.

1984

2
Samplers around the World

Sampler-making has played an important role in women's lives throughout history, and strong sampler-making traditions developed in a large number of countries around the world. These include France, Italy, Spain and the Spanish colonies, Mexico, Belgium, Scandinavia and Switzerland, with Britain, Germany, Holland and America holding the strongest traditions.

Each country retained its own national characteristics although there was much interplay of designs and patterns throughout Europe. The art of sampler-making crossed the Atlantic with the Pilgrim Fathers to the New World where it grew and flourished. In each country, sampler making followed similar developments through the centuries and underwent the same processes of gradual decline which accelerated from the mid-nineteenth century onwards, when samplers had lost their original purpose.

America

Samplers and the art of sampler-making came to America with the early settlers and most colonial women took their needlework very seriously. Mothers took great pride in their work and taught their daughters the art of stitching. The resulting samplers were hung in the parlour as proof of the daughter's ability to produce fine needlework. Darning, mending and marking were still important tasks in the home and girls were not considered marriageable until they had mastered the art of stitchery.

From the diary of Anna Green Winslow, written in 1771 and containing a record of a Boston school, comes the following account of a girl's duties for one day (9 March).

> A very snowy day. I have been a very good girl today about my work however . . . in the first place I sew'd on the bosom of uncle's shirt, mended two pairs of gloves, mended for the wash two handkerchiefs (one cambrick), sewed on half a border of a lawn apron of aunt's, read part of the XXIst chapter of Exodus and a story in the Mother's gift.

Original samplers, ideas and designs were brought to America from the old country and the first samplers made there reflected the national characteristics of the embroiderer's homeland. After 1750, there developed a distinctly American flavour to sampler-making. There was great imagination and flair in design, and the use of stitches, colours and different threads produced lively and distinctive works. Samplers became far less formal and symmetrical than British ones of the time.

The fabric used was usually unbleached linen, but light brown, bottle-green, grey and black were also used. Tiffany was also used until the early nineteenth century when linsey-woolsey (a mixture of flax and wool) became popular. Tammy was not as common as in Britain. Silk was by far the most popular thread, followed by wool and linen. In the eighteenth century, American sampler-makers made good, creative use of metal threads and spangles and worked pearl-stitched edgings and blackwork borders, though these slowly died out in the nineteenth century. Pattern-darning was often used to fill in backgrounds and through the clever use of simple stitches and colour, landscaped scenes appeared highly three-dimensional. Samplers were mounted and often framed, with silk-ribbon borders which were ruched, pleated or quilled; in some regions, gold braid or white satin damask was used.

Samplers in the second half of the eighteenth century generally consisted of a small square in which a verse or inscription was worked, surrounded by a very wide border which formed the major part of the work and was intended to be the main feature. Inside this border would be a landscaped scene with figures, trees, perhaps a dog, some sheep and winged cherubs. Large floral designs were often included, possibly worked up the sides of the border and with the sky at the top. Cross-band samplers were still being made around 1800, but were being replaced by the more pictorial types. The wide variety of stitches worked also diminished in the late eighteenth century and, as elsewhere in the world, cross stitch became the most popular stitch on samplers. A small number of lacework samplers were made in the late eighteenth century, especially in Philadelphia. These differed from the English pieces of the seventeenth century in

(*opposite*) American Fort and Animals (p70)

that they used pictorial designs rather than bands of patterning.

Mid-nineteenth-century Jewish samplers are instantly recognisable by the Hebrew alphabet and religious symbols, such as the spies of Canaan.

A group of samplers made in Pennsylvania by girls of German or Dutch ancestry are very different in character from other samplers being made in America. They were worked mostly in cross stitch and consisted of a roughly arranged collection of motifs. There were no borders, although the samplers were sometimes framed with silk ribbon. Among the different motifs worked were pairs of peacocks, flowers in vases, pointed stars, hearts and coronets, which were all similar to those appearing on European samplers.

Along with many other art forms, American samplers of the 1800s show the spirit of republicanism: many patriotic themes and emblems were worked onto them, including the American eagle with its wings outstretched. After the War of Independence, women's education had improved, although needlework still featured strongly in the school curriculum.

As in Britain, sampler-making was prominent in American educational establishments and both plain and fancy needlework were taught. Poor children learnt plain work and worked samplers of alphabets and numerals. The more adventurous pictorial pieces were made at fashionable ladies' seminaries and were intended to be framed. The very best samplers were worked by girls aged between twelve and sixteen years from the Boston area.

Reputations of schools were founded almost entirely on the standard, originality and style of the samplers being worked there, with each school developing its own individual characteristics of sampler design. These were largely decided by individual teachers, many of whom came from Britain.

Mrs Leah Meguier ran a school in Pennsylvania in the early nineteenth century, which produced very beautiful and imaginative samplers. They were often divided into as many as twenty-two 1in (2.5cm) squares, each containing a different motif or geometric pattern, including birds, flowers, butterflies, hearts and baskets of eggs. In the middle would be a scene which would include one or two figures, often a woman holding flowers. Weeping willows, often found in the area, were also popular. A few squares at the bottom would include an inscription or verse and quite often the name of the teacher was included. The following lines are typical of Pennsylvania verses:

This work of mine my friends may have
When I am dead and in my grave
This I did to let you see
What care my parents took of me.

Faces and figures in pictorial scenes were usually hand-painted and sequins were often used for further embellishment. The finished work was quite often framed with silk ribbon and gold lace.

Another well-known school was in Providence, Rhode Island, and was known as the Balch Academy. It was run by Miss Balch between 1785 and 1799 and took in both day and boarding girls. The samplers produced here had the major portion of the work as a landscaped scene, usually featuring large public buildings, often inside grand pillars. They were often heavily decorated with borders of large flowers growing out of urns and vases. Short inscriptions or verses were also included and the following are typical:

Honour and renown will be the ingenious crown.

May spotless innocence and truth
my every action guide
and guard my inexperienced youth
from arrogance and pride.

The stitches used were cross, stem, satin and rococo. Pattern-darning, which was usually diagonal, was often used to fill in backgrounds and was a main characteristic of the work from this school.

Westtown was a boarding school in Chester county which opened in 1799 and was supervised by the Quakers or the Society of Friends. It was one of the most distinguished seminaries in the country. The Quaker approach to education was sober and strict, and this was reflected in the samplers that were made there. Both boys and girls attended, but only the girls were taught the art of needlework; they learnt plain sewing such as mending, marking and darning. Later on, they were allowed to work samplers and globes. Map samplers were rare in America, probably due to the size of the country.

The earliest samplers worked at this school were very simple, often with vines and leaves worked into borders around alphabets and a few simple motifs. Coloured silks were used but, more often than not, samplers were worked in just black silk on linen. As in Britain, moral sentiments were expressed but here they were in the form of poems. Occasionally, more proficient workers were allowed to sew views of the school on samplers which would be framed, but in general this more adventurous work was frowned upon.

Like European blackwork samplers, this piece has been worked mostly in double running stitch. It is a Turkish sampler from the eighteenth or nineteenth century worked in silk on linen and measures 26 × 16½in (66 × 42cm). There are a large number of motifs which include many buildings, flowers and plants, all with a strong Eastern flavour. There are a few border patterns, but no animals *(Victoria and Albert Museum, London)*

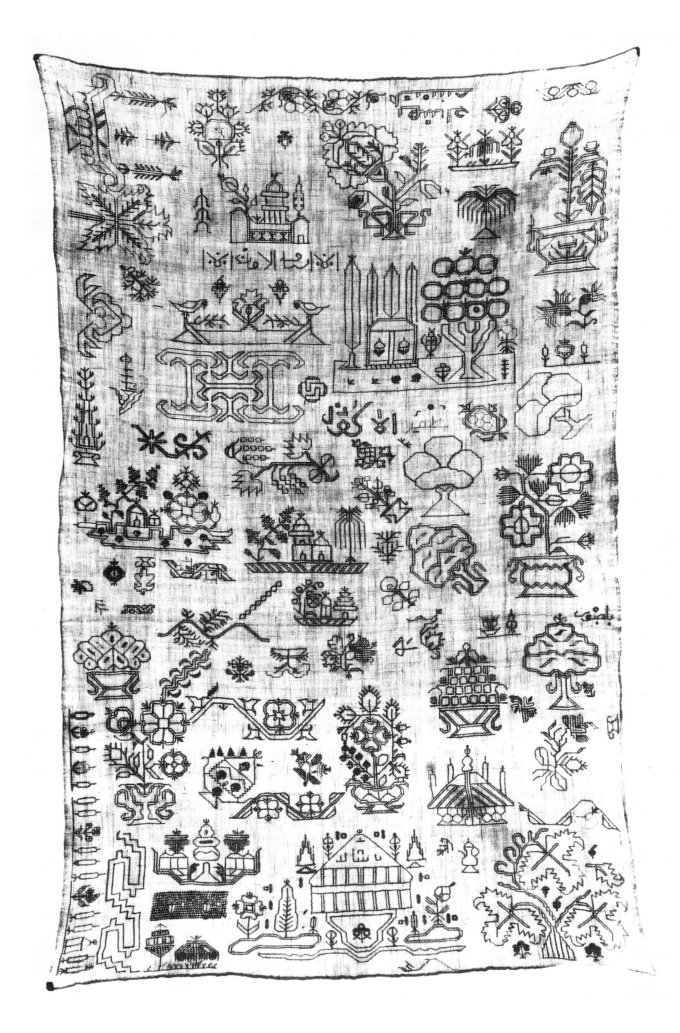

In the nineteenth century, samplers depicting family records or registers became very popular and remind us of how high the rate of infant mortality was, and of the strain that childbirth put on women bearing large numbers of children. Men often remarried two or three times. Some of these registers were in very plain work with a simple informative text surrounded by narrow borders. Others received much more elaborate treatment. The text was often worked inside an arch supported by columns and decorated with floral wreaths. Others were designed in the form of genealogical trees, with names and dates being worked inside fruits hanging from the branches.

Samplers were made in large numbers at the beginning of the nineteenth century but over the years the numbers and the standard of workmanship were to decline. By the mid-nineteenth century, samplers were being worked in wool and on a coarse canvas. These featured alphabets and numerals and were probably made by young girls. The craze for Berlin woolwork had effects on American embroidery in much the same way as in Britain, and the great age of the American sampler was now over.

Germany

From Germany, where the early publication of the first pattern books showed that the art of embroidery was well established, came great numbers of samplers.

A German sampler dated 1618 is thought to be the earliest dated example from the Continent, though there is evidence to suggest that samplers were being worked in Germany in the sixteenth century. Another early German sampler dated 1704 was made in Dölbeln, in Saxony, and consists of six various border patterns, two alphabets, numerals and a collection of small motifs near the bottom of the sampler, which include animals, flowers, birds and crowns. A small cartouche includes the initials of the worker and the whole is worked in cross stitch. The shape of this sampler is long and narrow and is similar to that of English seventeenth-century samplers. Samplers from Germany almost always include the initials of the worker and the date, although they are not often fully signed.

The shape of German samplers gradually became squarer, although they were occasionally rectangular; they were generally smaller than English samplers. There was no careful arrangement of motifs and alphabets in the early specimens, which usually included an alphabet, a number of designs and motifs scattered around the work.

Longer samplers of the eighteenth century were arranged more methodically, with lines of alphabets at the top, larger subjects in the middle and border patterns along the bottom. Those in the middle would often be religious scenes, which were very popular on German samplers of this period. These included representations of the crucifixion and the emblems of the Passion — the crown of thorns, sponge, hourglass, pincers, dice, cock, scourge, ladder, nails and hammer. Adam and Eve beneath the Tree of Knowledge and the serpent were also popular.

German samplers made at the beginning of the eighteenth century show a close resemblance to British samplers made in the first half of the century, being worked in cross stitch with motifs arranged symmetrically on the fabric. Borders were worked with various flowers, fruit and animals incorporated into the design, including roses, lilies, pinks, grapes, pears, deer and birds.

Alphabets were very popular and were worked in roman or rather ornate gothic styles. Short inscriptions or mottoes of a religious nature were preferred to text and verses. Houses and domestic scenes were not very common, but in the nineteenth century they did appear along with town gates, village scenes, furniture and animals, including lions, deer and parrots.

The finished sampler was usually mounted and edged with silk ribbon, often with the elaborate ruching also popular with American sampler-workers. It would be regarded as an heirloom to be kept in the family.

The repertoire of stitches used on German samplers was far more limited than on English ones; the earliest pieces were worked entirely in cross stitch, with the introduction of a few more stitches later on in the eighteenth century. Darning samplers were worked in Germany from very early times and were much more popular there than in England.

The early pieces showed restraint in the choice of colours, but after the middle of the nineteenth century, with the advances made in the production of aniline dyes, a very large selection of colours became available. The area of Vierlande near Hamburg developed characteristic samples which used just black thread on white linen.

Early samplers were worked on unbleached linen using silk or linen thread. As in Britain, tammy cloth came into fashion in the early nineteenth century and was available in narrow widths specially produced for sampler-making. Towards the end of the nineteenth century, samplers produced in schools were worked on a coarse canvas whilst others, which were probably worked at home, were sewn on cotton cambric.

The sampler was to remain the most popular way of teaching needlework to children in Germany, until the school curriculum was changed after the end of World War I and sampler-making was banned.

Holland

Dutch samplers are quite different in character from German examples, the shape generally being broader.

Another major distinction is that they are worked across the fabric, with the selvedges appearing at the sides of the sampler rather than at the top and the bottom. They are usually signed with the worker's initials and the date. Dutch samplers were produced in large numbers and included a huge variety of alphabets, designs and motifs, most of which had some religious significance. There was, however, an absence of any religious text or verses. Another strong characteristic of Dutch samplers are the very elaborately treated alphabets and numerals which were often worked in two or more colours and stitches.

The design and arrangement of these samplers are definitely patchy, with all sorts of motifs being loosely scattered around the material in a random fashion. Many of the subjects are religious and include the spies of Canaan, the now ubiquitous Adam and Eve, the five wise and five foolish virgins, many forms of the Tree of Life and the Virgin and Child, crosses and the sacred heart. Christ was depicted with the woman of Samaria at the well.

Cartouches and garlands are also included to contain dates and initials. Ships, mermaids, windmills and human figures are also quite popular. Other motifs range from buildings such as churches and houses, to household furniture, fruits, flowers, animals, birds and geometric motifs. A book published recently, *Embroidery Motifs from Dutch Samplers,* shows hundreds of designs, patterns, motifs and alphabets, and lists many of the meanings and translations which they are given. Dutch samplers were mainly worked in cross stitch but also made use of back stitch, bird's eye stitch and an open kind of satin stitch.

This Italian sampler was worked by Virginia Rocchi in the mid-nineteenth century. A pretty bouquet of flowers is worked in the centre; the alphabets are worked in cross stitch and Algerian eye. The border has been worked in a number of flowing floral patterns. The materials are silk on linen, and the sampler measures 13¾ × 20in (35 × 51cm) *(Victoria and Albert Museum, London)*

Some motifs appearing regularly on British samplers of the late seventeenth century were taken originally from Dutch samplers. I have noticed two designs in particular which originated from Holland and appear time and again on English samplers. These are a little scene with a stag seated underneath two trees and another with buildings which look like a chapel or school. The latter design has been used on the multiplication table project included in this book.

Spain

Spanish samplers were usually rather large and could be square or long in shape. They were generally sewn in silk, using striking colours in a very effective way. The material was almost entirely covered with a large variety of border patterns; as many as thirty different designs might be worked on one sampler. The patterns were totally geometric.

Early samplers were worked almost entirely in satin stitch, although cross and back stitches were occasionally used. Some Spanish samplers contained cut and drawn work. A very few pieces contained alphabets and these samplers, although rarely dated, were often signed in full. There are many Spanish samplers executed entirely in counted-thread work in one colour only, usually black. This was Spanish blackwork, a technique which became very popular in England.

Turkish and Moroccan samplers, which can be seen at the Victoria and Albert Museum in London, show patterns used for household linen; on one Moroccan sampler of the late eighteenth or early nineteenth century appear a number of borders which belong to European embroideries and pattern books of the first half of the sixteenth century.

Italy

Italy is the home of some very beautiful lacework. Italian cutwork and lacework were both great influences on Britain and the rest of Europe during the sixteenth and seventeenth centuries. Italian samplers of the seventeenth century contained lovely examples of cut and drawn work, with border patterns incorporating religious motifs which included the crucifixion and the symbols of the Passion. Italy also produced coloured samplers. A typical example from around 1800 was nearly square in shape and included alphabets and numerals, crosses, trees, figures and animals, and the fourteen emblems of the Passion.

France

Although the sampler does not seem to have been very popular in France, judging from the very few examples that have survived French samplers are beautifully fine. They were often worked on fine muslin and to a very high standard.

Most samplers were made by girls in convent schools and were perhaps practice pieces for skills to be employed in working ecclesiastical embroideries. The subjects were mainly religious and not usually pictorial. Many varied and subtle floral designs and borders were worked, some of which were much admired and copied on English pieces. These samplers did not include text or verses, and few workers gave their ages.

Other Countries

Swiss samplers displayed some very fine work but lacked vitality; whilst Belgium samplers closely resembled those from Germany, a much greater variety of stitches was used. Scandinavian samplers were usually worked on fine muslin and there are some lovely examples of Scandinavian drawn-thread work. In Denmark, when only the nobility were allowed to wear lace, other women developed a particular kind of embroidery that produced lacy effects. It was worked on cheesecloth initially, and later on fine muslin.

In India, where Anglo-Indian mothers taught their daughters the art of sampler-making and where some schooling existed in seminaries at Calcutta, samplers were worked under strong oriental influences. When combined with the European style, these influences produced some rather interesting and unique pieces.

An unsigned Danish sampler dated 1751. This more organised sampler has two figures in a landscaped scene surrounded by squares of patterning, which is again bordered by an arrangement of flowers and leaves. In the centre of the larger flowers appear some intriguing faces. The materials are silver-gilt thread, silk and wool on linen and the stitches include cross, tent, rococo, chain, eye, crosslet, brick and Florentine stitches, with padded and laid couched work. It measures 30½ × 26in (76 × 66cm) (*Victoria and Albert Museum, London*)

3
Symbols and Verses

Many art historians who have studied the symbolism of motifs appearing on decorative art forms have arrived at different conclusions. The mythology of ancient peoples from around the world, together with the use of motifs as heraldic emblems and religious symbols, naturally leads to some confusion in interpretation. Most motifs will have some kind of religious significance as well as being derived from ancient legends or folklore; some are simply renditions of everyday items and have no particular meaning. I have included here a few of the most popular interpretations of the many different birds, beasts, fruits, flowers and trees which are depicted on samplers through the centuries and from around the world.

Flowers

The rose is often called the flower of love, beauty and joy and it was a very early pagan symbol signifying earthly love. It was also a symbol of Venus, of Dionysus and of Bacchus, and became the flower of divine love when seen with the Virgin Mary. Five roses on a bush are said to represent the blood of the martyrs. In the Middle Ages, the rose was a symbol of the mystic vision, of courtly love and of the female pudenda. Because of its popularity in English gardens of the time, the rose became the national emblem of the Tudor kings and has appeared frequently on English samplers.

The carnation originated in the Far East and its name was derived from the Latin *carnis,* meaning flesh (the first carnation was flesh coloured). It is supposed to represent maternal love, and, when connected with the Virgin Mary, it has similar meanings to the rose.

The tulip, often called the symbol of perfect love, originated in the East. A Persian legend tells of how a young man, rejected by the girl he loved, cried in the desert. When his tears fell to the ground they turned into tulips. The tulip shape is similar to that of the chalice and also has a religious significance.

A lily is said to have sprung up where Eve dropped a tear on leaving Eden, and the white Madonna lily is said to have been yellow when the Virgin Mary stooped to pick it up. It is known as the flower of heaven, symbolising purity or chastity, and is some-

times thought to represent the Redeemer or the saints and the kingdom of heaven. In some eastern countries it is a symbol of fertility. It is sometimes thought that the fleur-de-lys was derived from the lily and that this was further stylised into the Prince of Wales' feathers, although these two designs could well have been inspired by the iris.

Both the violet and the daisy are said to be the flowers of humility, while the marigold represents obedience and is one of the flowers of the sun. The honeysuckle represents enduring faith, and, as a garden flower, is supposed to have power to avert the evil eye. It was a firm favourite with the Tudors.

The cowslip, or herb peter, is said to symbolise the keys of Saint Peter; the columbine is said to symbolise the Holy Spirit as it closely resembles the shape of a dove. The pansy, or love-in-idleness, with its three faces in the sacred trefoil shape, represents the Holy Trinity, as its Latin name, *Herba trinatis,* suggests.

Fruits

The Latin word for apple, *malum,* also means evil, to denote Christianity's forbidden fruit. In folklore, the apple was offered as a gift, a declaration of love. It was also the symbol of love and fertility because of its beauty and sweetness. The pear also appears regularly on samplers and embroideries and is sometimes considered more likely than the apple to have been the forbidden fruit.

Grapes have a strong religious significance and represent the blood of Jesus. A bunch of grapes being carried by the spies of Canaan is often seen on samplers through the centuries. The cherry is considered to be another of the fruits of heaven. The strawberry represents perfect righteousness, as it is considered the perfect fruit, having no stones or pips. The leaves have a shape similar to the sacred trefoil, giving the strawberry religious significance. The white flowers are said to indicate innocence and purity.

Ancient Hebrews used the pomegranate embroidered on religious garments and the fruit was said to have inspired the design of Solomon's crown. It has been considered the emblem of the Christian Church and its religious meaning is hope of eternal life. It was used as a heraldic emblem in the sixteenth century and appeared regularly on samplers of this time. It also features in Chinese poetry and in the Near East its abundance of seeds symbolises fertility. In Greek legend, Ceres' daughter Persephone had to spend half of every year underground because she ate one pomegranate seed while in Hades.

Trees

The Tree of Knowledge was the tree heavily laden with the fruit of the knowledge of good and evil, which ultimately led to the Fall. It is commonly depicted on samplers with the clad or unclad figures of Adam and Eve, and often with the serpent.

The Tree of Life has, through the ages, been depicted in many different ways. In Egypt, the gods are said to have lived in its branches and survived on its fruit — 'the bread of life'. In Persia, the Tree of Life bore all the seeds for living plants, to be scattered by the birds which are often depicted around the tree. In ancient Hindu writings the tree is considered a divine mother and a bearer of life: the progress and growth of a tree planted after the birth of a baby is said to determine that of the child. The Tree of the Universe was believed to have been an ash tree and was the symbol of the Universe.

The weeping willow tree appears regularly on later samplers, being especially popular with American sampler-makers. It is traditionally the tree of sorrow. The olive has religious significance, representing peace and good will. The oak tree has played an important role in British mythology since its popularity with the druids, and was further promoted by Charles II who hid in an oak tree when fleeing from the government's army. It appeared often as a heraldic emblem, and both acorns and oak leaves were worked into patterns on samplers.

Birds, Animals and Insects

Dove: A symbol of the Holy Ghost, representing mercy and peace; a dove with a letter in its beak is a messenger of love.
Duck: Marital fidelity.
Unicorn: A symbol of chastity and purity; also a sign of the Redeemer.
Goose: Watchfulness and stupidity.
Cock: A symbol of Christ, and of watchfulness and penitence.
Hare: Faintheartedness, timidity and flight.
Hart: Gentleness and pride.

Dog: Watchfulness and fidelity.
Cat: Idleness and coquetry.
Stork: Parental love.
Parrot: Talkativeness and gossip.
Peacock: Vanity, immortality and eternal life.
Tortoise: Strength.
Snake: Reward and wickedness.
Falcon: Pride and nobility.
Butterfly: Joy, pleasure and immortality.
Swan: The bird of love, a symbol of a good death. In German mythology it is the creature of the sun, the bringer of light and life.
Lion: Strength and steadfastness.
Monkey: The devil, the antithesis of the Virgin.
Owl: Sometimes represents the devil and avarice; alternatively it can represent wisdom and learning due to its connections with Athena the goddess of wisdom.
Squirrel: Mischief.
Horse: A symbol of the sun, male potency and fertility; also pride, speed and ardour.
Bee: A symbol of chastity.

Verses

Apart from the many pieces of religious text that were included on later samplers, a very large number of verses were also worked. They prove a fascinating insight into the social history of the time. We can read of the great importance placed on needlework and of the Victorians' obsession with the subject of death. Many verses were highly moralistic, others expounded on the woman's role, and although these may seem rather amusing, I am sure that at the time they were seriously meant. The verses for children are quite charming and could still be worked today. Those concerning needlework and for parents are also still relevant. A sampler that has been worked specially to celebrate an occasion or dedicated to a particular person is of very great value. A verse or piece of text included in a sampler together with as much information as possible (your name, the date and where it was made etc) will add special interest to the piece, creating something that will be treasured for a very long time.

The following verses are just a few of the more interesting ones that I have seen worked on samplers; I hope some of them will be worked again, although you may wish to use another favourite piece of text that would be relevant to a particular sampler.

To Parents

This work of mine my friends may have
When I am dead and in my grave
This I did to let you see
What care my parents took of me.

On this Fair Canvas does my needle write
With Love and Duty both this I indite
And in these lines dear Parent I impart
The tender feelings of a Grateful Heart.

My mother hatherto hath don her best to make
me a work woman as well as the rest
Anne Iater is my name and England is my nation
and south work is my dwelling place and
Christ is my salvation

Dear mother I am young and cannot show
Such work as I unto your goodness owe
Be pleased to smile on this my small endeavour
I'll strive to learn and be obedient forever.

Many daughters have done virtuously
But thou excellest them all.

Lord thou wast pleased to bestow on me a Mother truly
kind,
Whose constant care was to instil good precepts on my
mind:
And plant the seeds of virtue in my young and tender
breast.
Ere thou didst snatch her from my sight with thee to be
at rest.
Grant me O Lord thy constant aid to thy holy will.
That a tender Mothers pious wish may be in me fulfilled.

Oh smile on those whose liberal care
Provides for our instruction here;
And let our conduct ever prove
We're grateful for their generous love.

Next unto God dear parents I address
Myself to you in humble thankfulness
For all your care and charge on me bestowed
The means of learning unto me allowed
Go on I pray and let me still pursue
Those golden arts the friendless never knew

Verses for Children

The trees were green,
The sun was hot,
Sometimes I worked,
And sometimes not.
Seven years my age,
My name Jane Grey,
and often much,
Too fond of play.

Angels are happy clothed with wings
But our new Cloaths are dangerous things
The child well drest had need to be aware
Lest her fine raiment prove a snare
But happy children they whose dress
Is the redeemer's righteousness
Ere long in glory they shall shine
Rob'd in that raiment all divine

Jesus permit thy gracious name to stand
As the first effort of an infant hand
And while her fingers on the canvas move
Incline her tender heart to seek thy love
With thy dear children let her have a part.

Dear child delay no time
But with all speed amend
The longer thou dost live
The nearer to thy end
Oh child most dear
Incline thy ear
And hearken to God's voice.

Sweet it is to see a child
Tender, merciful and mild
Eveready to perform
Acts of kindness to a worm.

Poetic

I am like the lonesome dove
That mourns its absent mate
From hill to hill from vale to vale
Its sorrows to relate
But Caanaane land is just before
Sweet spring is coming on
A few more beating winds and rains
And winter will be gone

Catch the sunshine, don't be grieving
O'er that darksome billow there
Life's a sea of stormy billows,
We must meet them everywhere.
Pass right through them, do not tarry
Overcome the heaving tide,
There's a sparkling gleam of sunshine
Waiting on the other side.

38

A Woman's Role

Adam alone in Paradise did grieve
And thought Eden a desert without Eve
Until God, pitying his lonesome state
Crown'd all his wishes with a lovely mate
Then why should men think mean or slight her
That could not live in Paradise without her.

A silent and loving woman is a gift of the Lord and there
is nothing so much worth as a mind well instructed.

She who is truly polite knows how to
contradict with respect and please without
adulation, is equally remote from insipid
complaisance and low familiarity.

One did commend to me a WIFE both fair and young
That had French Spanish and Italian Tongue
I thanked him kindly and told him I loved none such
For I thought one tongue for a Wife too much
What love ye not the Learned, Yes as my life
A Learned Scholar but not a Learned Wife.

With cheerful mind we yield to men
The higher honours of the pen
The needles our great care,
In this we chiefly wish to shine
How far the art's already mine
This Sampler does declare.

Religious Verses

.... is my name
America is my nation
.... is my dwelling place
And Christ is my salvation.

See how the lilies flourish white and fair
See how the ravens fed from heaven are,
Then ne'er distrust the God for cloth and bread
Whilst lilies flourish and the ravens fed.

Seek to be good instead of great and
Sing my makers praise.

The Holy Feast of Easter was injoined
To bring Christ's Ressurrection to our mind.
Rise then from Sin as He did from the Grave
That by His Merrits he Your Souls may save.

How blest are they who in their Prime
the paths of truth have early trod,
Who yield the first fruits of their time
And consecrate their youth to God.

Concerning Needlework

In the glad morn of blooming youth
These various threads I drew,
And now behold this finished piece
Lies glorious to the view.
So when bright youth shall charm no more
And age shall chill my blood,
May I review my life and say,
Behold my works are good.

In reading this if any faults you see
Mend them yourself and find no fault in me.

.... worked this in great speed
And left it here for you to read.

When I was young
And in my prime
Here you may see
How I spent my time.

Of female arts in usefulness
The needle far exceeds the rest,
In ornament there's no device
Affords adorning half so nice.

How blest the Maid whom circling years improve
Her God the object of her warmest love
Whose active years successive as they glide
The Book, the Needle and the Pen divide.

On Virtues

Learn little maid, each useful art
Which may adorn thy youth.
Learn to improve thy tender heart
In virtue, Grace and truth.
Shun every vice with studied care
Each female folly flee
That every grace that crowns the fair
May all attend on thee.

Vain is alike the joy we seek,
And vain what we possess,
Unless harmonious Reason tunes
The passions into peace.
To temper'd wishes just desires,
Is happiness confin'd,
And, deaf to folly's call, attends
The music of my mind.

Humility I'd recommend
Good nature, too, with ease,
Be generous, good and kind to all,
You'll never fail to please.

The bird which soars on highest wing
Builds on the ground her lowly nest;
And she that doth most sweetly sing
Sings in the shade when all things rest.
In lark and nightingale we see
What honour hath humility.

Contented with my humble state I
will pass my peaceful days

If I am right, Oh teach my heart
Still in the right to stay,
If I am wrong, thy grace impart
To find that better way.

When wealth to virtuous hands is given
It blesses like the dews of heav'n
Like heav'n it hears the orphan's cries
And wipes the tears from widows eyes.

Health Seems a Cherub Most Divinely bright,
More Soft than Air, More gay than Morning Light,
Hail, blooming Goddess, thou propitious power,
Whose blessings Mortals Next to Life implore,
Such Graces in your Heavenly Eyes appear
That Cottages are Courts, when you are there.

On Friendship

In prosperity friends are plenty
In adversity not one in twenty.

Declare thy secret thought to none,
For fear of shame and sorrow.
For he that is your friend to-day
May be the foe to-morrow.

Return the kindness that you do receive
As far as your ability gives leave
Keep such company as you may improve
or that may improve you

Be you unto others kind and true
As you'd have others be to you,
And never do or say to men
What'er you would not take again

Tell me ye knowing and discerning few
Where I may find a friend both firm and true
Who dares stand by me when in deep distress
And this his love and friendship most express.

Words of Caution

Learn to contemn all praise betimes
For flattery is the Nurse of Crimes
With early Virtue plant thy Breast
The Specious Arts of Vice detest
Regard the world with cautious eye
Nor raise your expectations high
See that the balanced scale be such
You neither fear nor hope too much

With soothing wiles he won my easy heart
He sigh'd and vow'd, but oh he feigned the smart;
Sure of all friends the blackest we can find
Are those ingrates who stab our peace of mind

Sweetly blooms the rose of May
Glitt'ring with the tears of morn
So insideous smiles betray
While they hide the treacherous thorn

What is the blooming tincture of the skin
To peace of mind and harmony within?
What is the bright sparkling of the finest eye,
To the soft soothing of a calm reply?
Can comeliness of form, or shape, or air,
With comeliness of words or deeds compare?
No — Those at first the unwary heart may gain,
But these — these only, can the heart retain.
And you, ye fair with cautious arm
'Gainst Man's perfidious Arts,
For Youth and Beauty vainly charm
When virtue once departs

Short Moralistic Lines

My time at school well spent
I never shall repent

A house divided against itself can't stand

'Tis education forms the common mind;
Just as the twig is bent the tree's inclined.

Zeal in a good cause will merit applause.

To wisdom's counsel lend an ear,
true godliness to gain.

That which will not make a pot may make a pot lid

He who spends all he gets is on the road to want.

A small hole will sink a great ship.

Time cut them all
Both great and small.

A diligent Scholar is an ornament to a School

Concerning Death

When I can read my title clear
to mansions in the skies,
I'll bid farewell to every fear
And wipe my weeping eyes.

Fragrant the rose, but it fades in time
The violet sweet, but quickly past the prime
White lillies hang their heads and soon decay
And whiter snow in minutes melts away
Such and so with'ring are our early joys
Which time or sickness speedily destroys.

No longer I follow a sound
No longer a dream I pursue
O happiness now to be found
Unobtainable treasure Adieu.

Our life is never at a stand
'Tis like a fading flower
Death which is always near at hand
Comes nearer every hour

When I am dead and worms me eat
Here you shall see my name complete.

There is an hour when I must die
Nor can I tell how soon twill come
A thousand children young as I
Are called by death to hear their doom.

Redeem the mispent time thats past
And live each day as it were thy last
And of thy talents take great care
For thy last day thyself prepare

The rising morning can't assure
That we shall end the day
For death stands ready at the door
To take our lives away.

Ye friends of my heart
Ere from you I depart
This hope to my breast is most near
If again we shall meet
In this rural retreat
May we meet as we part with a tear.

May no marble bestow
The splendour of woe
Which the children vanity rear
No fiction of fame
Shall blazon my name
All I ask is a wish is a tear.

Lillies blended with the rose
Now no more adorn her face
Nor her Cheek with Blushes glow
Adding Charms to every grace.

O may I seize the transient hour
Improve each moment as it flies
Life a short summer man a flower
He dies Alas how soon he dies.

Mother dear weep not for me
When in this yard my grave you see
My time was short and blest was he
That called me to eternity

When spring appears, when violets grow,
And shed a rich perfume,
How soon the fragrance breathes its last
How short lived is the bloom?

4
Making a Sampler

Most types of embroidery need the support of some kind of frame whilst they are being worked, as this prevents distortion and helps to achieve neater stitchery. All the projects should be worked on one of the types of frame described below.

Hoops

These are two rings, usually of wood, in between which the fabric is sandwiched. The outer ring is then tightened by a small screw and the fabric is held taut. The hoop must be larger than the intended embroidery. Hoops are available in a number of sizes, the largest being of a heavier weight and quite sturdy. Hoops are preferred for small pieces of embroidery on lightweight fabrics.

Frames

There are a number of different kinds, the best being those which are square and large enough to take the complete embroidery without the need for rolling up the work. Some frames with floor stands are available.

Needles

Only blunt-ended needles should be used for counted-thread work; sharp-ended needles will pierce both the threads of the fabric and any embroidered threads already worked. This will mean distorted stitches which will not lie neatly. The size of the needle used should relate to the size of the threads, the thread count and the thickness of the thread to be worked.

Scissors

Embroidery scissors are fine and sharp. Dressmaking scissors should be used for cutting the fabric, but dressmaker's 'unpickers' should never be used. Scissors intended for embroidery or dressmaking should never be used for cutting paper, as this will blunt them.

Fabric

All the fabrics I have used for the projects are sold specially for counted-thread work and are commonly available in needlework shops and large department stores with a fabric department. Fabric is sold labelled with the number of holes (threads) to the square inch or centimetre — this is the thread count and varies greatly. The fewer the number of holes to the square inch or centimetre, the larger a piece of counted-thread embroidery will be. There are many different sorts of fabrics available, made in different yarns, with different finishes, textures and colours; these factors, together with the thread count, are all important when designing an embroidery.

Plain-weave Fabric

This is usually tightly woven with a smooth surface and a single weave; some varieties are available on which it is possible to count the threads for counted-thread embroidery. The number of threads for the warp and the weft will not usually be the same on plain-weave fabrics.

Evenweave Fabric

This is also fabric with a plain, single weave, but the number of threads for the warp and the weft are the same. The texture is open and the threads are easily counted. Popular types available are fine white and coloured linens, cambric, Glenshee and Glamis.

Hardanger

This differs from the evenweave fabrics in that it has pairs of threads intersecting. I have found this most effective for blackwork embroidery as the threads are very easy to count and the fabric remains firm, keeping its shape better than a single-weave fabric. Hardanger is available in a number of colours.

Binca

Like hardanger, this is another multiweave fabric, usually with interlaced groups of four threads.

Canvas

This is the name given to any kind of fabric in which the threads are tightly spun and woven with a space between them. It comes in different qualities, colours and widths, and the thread count varies. Canvas can be bought in a single or a double mesh. A locked-weave canvas has two weft yarns twisted together with the warp, which greatly reduces distortion and is much preferred. It is always wise to work on good-quality canvas — it is not only easier to work on but also produces much better results. Synthetic canvases should be avoided. Canvas is sold in white, bleached white, and a number of darker colours.

Threads
There is an enormous variety of threads available for embroidery purposes. I have used some of the most popular ones for the projects in this book.

Stranded Cottons
Anchor Stranded Cottons and DMC Stranded Cottons are both well-known brands consisting of six strands of cotton twisted together loosely which can be separated into groups of the required number, so giving different thicknesses. They are available in an enormous range of colours.

Coton Perlé
This is available in a number of brands and a large range of colours. It is a twisted two-ply thread with a high sheen.

Coton à Broder
This is a single (or three-strand) thread made by Coats and is equivalent to about two strands of the above stranded cottons. It is available in a fairly large number of colours.

Bella Donna
This is a silky thread made from 100 per cent viscose and comes in a number of colours. It has a high sheen and can produce some lovely effects with different stitches. It is, however, difficult to work and very slippery, the ends tending to fluff up rather quickly.

Wool
Wools are available in a number of qualities and weights. Generally, the larger the thread count, the thicker the yarn should be. There are two types of wool used for embroidery: those which are intended to be worked whole and those which are made up of a number of strands which can be separated into either a single strand, or several strands.

All embroidery wools are worsted yarns, which means that they are made with wool of a long staple and spun with plenty of twist. The staples or hairs of the wool are spun in one direction. To avoid damaging the yarn, it must be threaded so that the wool is pulled through the canvas in the direction in which it was spun.

The thickness of the yarn or the number of strands which are used should remain constant unless otherwise stated. Different brands of yarn all vary in thickness, so it is advisable to work a whole embroidery using colours from just one particular brand of wool.

Different dyes affect wool in various ways and you may find that the thickness of certain colours varies. If the yarn is not of a sufficient thickness to cover the ground properly, an extra strand may have to be included.

Tension Guide
The following guide is intended to help you find the correct thickness of thread to use with the many different weights of fabric which are available. The information given is based on the assumption that the principal stitches to be used are either cross or tent stitches.

The figures given here are approximate, and as all embroiderers work at different tensions it is wise to experiment with the threads and fabrics before beginning a piece of embroidery. Try a small test area of stitching using both cross and tent stitches. You will then be able to judge whether or not the thread is of the correct thickness for the fabric you are using. The resulting stitches must not be bulky or difficult to work, nor must they be too thin. When working with wool on canvas, the stitches must cover the ground sufficiently.

Evenweave Lightweight Fabrics
For a thread count of 18 to 22 holes to 1in (2.5cm): coton perlé.
20 to 23 holes to 1in (2.5cm): four strands of stranded cotton.
24 to 30 holes to 1in (2.5cm): three strands of stranded cotton.
27 to 40 holes to 1in (2.5cm): two strands of stranded cotton.
24 to 28 holes to 1in (2.5cm): coton à broder.
All these figures are for working cross stitch over two threads.

Canvas
For a thread count of 7 to 9 pairs of threads to 1in (2.5cm): Coats Tapisserie Wool, using cross stitch, over one pair of threads.
14 to 18 holes to 1in (2.5cm) (single mesh): Coats Tapisserie Wool, using cross stitch, over two threads.
12 holes to 1in (2.5cm) (single mesh): Coats Tapisserie Wool using tent stitch, over a single thread.
12 to 14 pairs of threads to 1in (2.5cm): two strands of embroidery wool using tent stitch over one pair of threads.

Size and Preparation of Fabric
If you are following the instructions for one of the projects in this book, you will need fabric at least 8in (20cm) larger on all four sides than the completed sampler. If you are designing your own, you need to calculate the size of the intended work and then add

43

(cont on p49)

centre

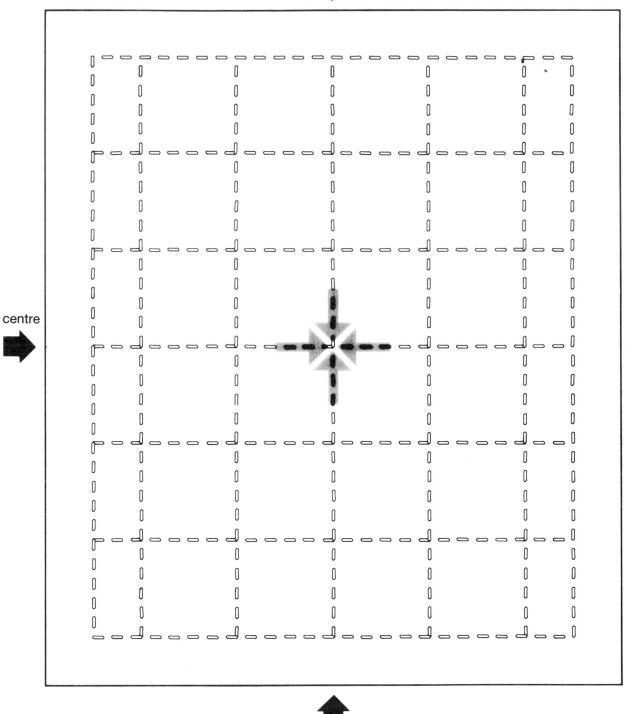

Fig 1   Guidelines. Lines of tacking outline the total area to
be worked, indicate the centre of the sampler, and divide
the piece into squares of 20/25 stitches

(*opposite*) Trees, Flowers and Birds (p77)
(*overleaf*) Alphabets and Border Patterns (p85); Wedding
Celebration (p76)

1985

Emily Don Aged 11years.

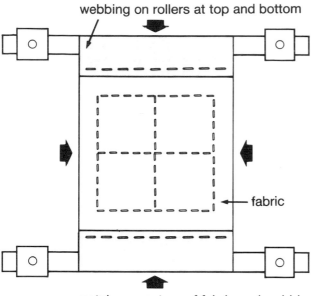

webbing on rollers at top and bottom

fabric

match up centres of fabric and webbing

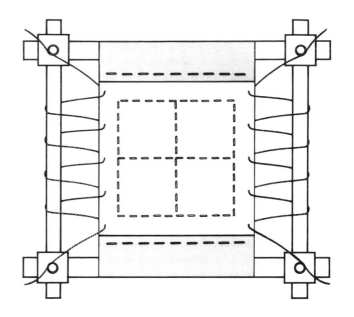

Fig 2 Mounting fabric onto a frame

the extra 8in (20cm) all round. To do this you need to know the thread count, that is, the number of threads per inch (2.5cm) of the fabric. Work out the number of stitches horizontally across the sampler, and also from top to bottom. Multiply the number of stitches across the work by the number of threads over which you intend to work each stitch (in cross stitch this is generally two). This will give you the number of threads to be worked over. Divide this figure by the thread count and this will give you the total width in inches or centimetres. Repeat these calculations for the length of the sampler.

Before cutting the fabric to the required size, remember that the selvedges are generally placed at the sides of the sampler. This is especially important when working with fabrics that are not of an even weave, that is, when the number of threads to the inch (2.5cm) is not the same across both the warp and the weft.

When cutting the fabric, you may find it easier to pull a whole length of thread from the fabric along the line you intend to cut.

Guidelines (see page 44)
Before starting a sampler it is advisable to work guidelines of tacking stitches in a brightly coloured thread. These act as very useful markers to help with the correct positioning of the designs and motifs. They are vital when working lines of text, as they help prevent the lettering from wandering from the correct lines of threads. Guidelines can be worked above and below lines of lettering and if you follow these very carefully they will prove a great help.

(*opposite*) Child Holding a Rabbit (p84)

Before mounting the fabric onto the frame, find the centre of the fabric by folding it in half both lengthwise and across the width. Where the two folds meet, work a small stitch — this marks the centre. The first guidelines should be for the length down and the width across the centre of the fabric. Count very carefully, working from the centre out. Further guidelines may be worked to form a grid across the fabric. Pencil in on the chart corresponding lines, perhaps twenty or twenty-five squares apart. Finish with a line all around the outer limit of the proposed sampler. Remember that each square on the chart represents one stitch and not one thread or hole. When you have finished, it is wise to check again that your lines are in exactly the right place — any mistakes will lead to a great deal of confusion.

Mounting Fabric onto an Embroidery Frame
This method should not be used for those frames which require a portion of the work to be rolled up; a square frame large enough to take the whole area to be worked without the need for rolling up is preferred.

After working tacking-stitch guidelines, fold over 1in (2.5cm) on all sides and hem lightly. With the selvedges at the sides, sew webbing tape along both sides. For heavier canvas it is not necessary to hem the edges or to use webbing. The edges can simply be sealed with a heavy tape.

Now sew the top of the fabric to the webbing on the top arm of the frame, making sure that the centres of the fabric and the frame are matched up. Repeat this for the bottom of the fabric and the frame. Assemble the complete frame, rolling up any excess fabric at the

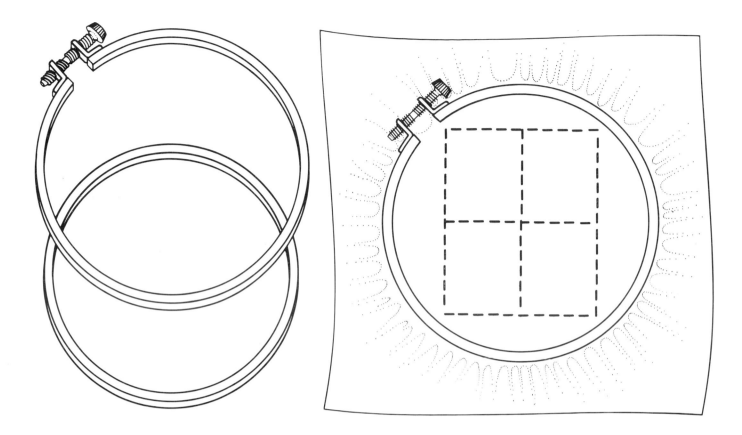

Fig 3 Mounting fabric in a hoop. The larger ring is placed on top of the right side of the fabric, and the smaller ring is placed underneath

top and the bottom. With strong thread, lace through the webbing at the sides of the fabric and around the sides of the frame. The lacing should be pulled tightly enough to stretch the fabric across the frame, and the top and bottom of the frame should be adjusted to stretch the fabric vertically. The fabric should now be firmly and evenly stretched on the frame. From time to time as the sampler progresses, it will be necessary to adjust both the lacing and the frame to ensure that the fabric remains properly stretched.

Mounting Fabric onto a Hoop

The hoop used should be large enough to take the whole area to be worked; it should never be placed *over* stitching. The inner hoop can be covered with white bias binding which will help to stop the fabric from slipping and prevent it from being distorted. Wrap the tape around the edges of the hoop, covering it completely. Place the fabric in position over the inner hoop. Loosen the screw on the outer hoop and place over the fabric and the inner hoop. Tighten the screw slightly and adjust the fabric, making sure that it is in position and that it is square. Continue to tighten the screw until the two hoops are locked together, ensuring that the fabric is stretched firmly across the hoop.

Preparing the Threads

The length of the thread to be used should not be longer than 18in (46cm); anything longer may twist and tangle. Wool may start wearing thin, cottons will lose any sheen they may have and the textures of threads such as coton perlé, gold and silver, may suffer.

Wool

Wool is spun in one direction, with the staples or individual hairs being twisted from one end. The wool should be pulled through the fabric in the same direction as it was spun so as not to pull the staples the wrong way. You can feel this by running your finger and thumb up and down the thread.

Stranded wool should be stripped, the strands separated and the required number placed together.

Stranded Cottons

These too should be stripped into individual strands and the required numbers put together.

Using the Charts

There are no definite rules about where to start. In my experience each sampler is different. If there is a piece of text or an alphabet to be included it would be wise to work that first; otherwise begin with the focal point of the sampler, or the largest motif to be worked. I usually sew the border last. The guidelines marked on the charts should be used to achieve the correct placing of the different motifs and designs. You might find it helpful to shade over lightly with a pencil the areas on the charts that have been worked.

Each square on the chart represents one stitch and not one thread or hole. A symbol inside a square represents a stitch worked in a particular colour, which is indicated in the colour key given with each project. An empty square, unless otherwise stated, represents unworked ground. Areas representing satin stitch may be shaded on the charts, and unless otherwise stated a stitch is worked into every hole and over the number of threads shown on the chart. In some projects you will need to work closely with charts and colour photographs to match stitches and colours, and there is certainly scope for using your own ideas/ colours etc. It would be wise for beginners to start with those projects using only one stitch throughout (eg Projects 1, 2 and 3).

Working in Ends
Work the first stroke of the first stitch to emerge at the front of the work, leaving a length of about 3in (7.5cm) spare at the back of the work. Begin working the stitches and at the same time hold the thread remaining at the back of the work in such a position that it is covered by the reverse strokes of the stitches being worked, so weaving it into the under side of the work. Do this for about ½in (1cm) and then cut away the excess. When you wish to finish the thread, you can use the same method to secure both the end of one thread and the beginning of the next. Ends of threads can be woven into the reverse of existing stitches, though you may feel that this distorts the front of the stitches. This distortion should not happen if a blunt-ended needle is used, because the threads will not be pierced by the needle.

Stitching
When working a group or solid area of stitches, remember that the needle should be brought up to the front of the work through unworked ground, and down through holes where stitches have already been worked. This rule should be followed wherever possible and with a little forethought and planning, stitching should be straightforward.

If your thread develops a lot of twist as you work, let the needle and the thread hang freely from your work, so allowing the thread to untwist. Other problems may be caused by using too great a length of thread.

If your stitching seems lumpy and uneven, the thread may be too thick — see page 43 for a guide to thread thicknesses and weights of fabrics. Correct mounting of the fabric onto the frame or hoop is also an important factor.

Borders and Turning Corners
If you are designing your own sampler, always plan your design on graph paper first, making careful calculations as to how many stitches your design will require.

Draw the border pattern onto the graph paper, beginning at the very centre of one side of the sampler. Work to the top, stopping at a suitable distance away from the sides of the work.

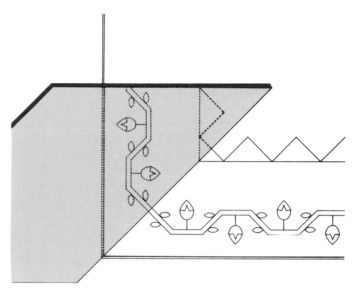

Fig 4   How to turn a corner in a border

There are several different ways of treating the corners of borders. The most common is to turn the 90° angle in mirror fashion. Hold a flat-edged mirror (one that is not bevelled and not in a frame) vertically to the graph paper, at 45° to the line of border patterning. The mirror should be touching the paper exactly where you wish to turn the border. Now look into the mirror and you will see your border pattern reversed in the mirror and travelling across the top of the planned sampler, forming a perfectly symmetrical turn in the pattern. By moving the mirror backwards and forwards, you will see the endless possible variations of turning the border at different points along the repeat of the pattern.

By placing the whole border a little higher or lower, you can also alter the width and length of the sampler until it suits the design as a whole or enables you to fit in the necessary motifs, alphabets etc.

The corners of border patterns do not necessarily have to be symmetrical, but it is important to end up with a well-balanced design. The Wedding Celebration project (8) has a border of flowers which is not perfectly symmetrical but looks right. The Multiplication Table (13) has patterned squares at the corners where the border pattern finishes. The small Rabbit sampler (19) has a bow in one corner.

Lettering and Text

The arrangement of lettering on a sampler can seem daunting, but it only needs a little time and patience. You will need to chart out the letters and text onto graph paper first, having decided upon the exact words you wish to include; do not forget the punctuation marks.

There are several tricks which can be used to make lettering fit neatly into an area. The spaces between each word can be shortened or lengthened, or you can change a particular word to another shorter or longer word with the same meaning; for example, 'worked', 'sewn' and 'embroidered' all mean the same. Names can be worked in full, using just initials or with initial and surname: Sarah Don, S.D. or S. Don. Dates and numerals can also be in words or figures, but try to remain consistent in the use of initials or numerals throughout the work.

Small symbols or short pieces of simple border patterns can be worked at the ends of rows of lettering to fill up any spaces that are left. Crowns and hearts have been traditionally used for this purpose. A tiny pattern or motif can be used instead of spacing in between each word.

The use of tacking stitches as guidelines is most important; these are placed at the top and bottom of the lines of text to prevent them from 'wandering'.

If you are familiar with the style of the alphabet you are using, you can work out how long and over how many stitches and threads a word or number of words will be. Count the number of stitches for each letter of each word. Allow another stitch between each letter of each word and (generally) four stitches between each word. The total will give you the number of stitches which a line of text will cover, and, depending on how many threads your stitches are worked over, the number of threads.

Simple lines of border patterns or satin stitch can be used to divide lines of text, and can take the place of punctuation marks. Words can be in capitals or in lower case, or the first letter of each word can be in capitals and the remainder in lower case. Script can also be used.

Complete sets of alphabets and numerals are given after the projects, page 135. They are numbered for easy reference, and each project has information on which sets to use where relevant.

Golden Rules of Embroidery

There are many strict rules to be followed when working a piece of embroidery. The following rules were definitely not made to be broken!

Never use an 'unpicker' to cut through stitches that have to be unpicked.
Never start a new thread with a knot to secure the end.
Do not press counted-thread embroidery — it will be completely flattened and lifeless.
Do not fold your work; always store it flat and never in coloured tissues. Use white, acid-free tissue paper.
The needle must never be left in the fabric; in time it will distort the fabric and may rust, leaving a nasty stain.
Do not leave the work rolled up on a frame for any length of time — loosen the roller or hoop until you are ready to start working again.

Mounting and Framing

Having removed the finished sampler from the frame or hoop, make sure that all the edges are neatly hemmed with a border of not more than 4in (10cm) outside the finished edges of the stitched area. Carefully measure across and down the embroidered area of the work at the widest points. Cut a piece of very thick strong card ½-1in (12-25mm) larger all round than this, making sure that it is perfectly square. A large set square will be necessary. The extra card will partly disappear into the picture frame. If more space is preferred around the work, allow the appropriate measurement on the edges when measuring the card.

Cut a double layer of muslin 1½-2in (3.5-5cm) larger than the card. Stretch this firmly over the card and secure to the back with masking tape. Place the embroidery over the card and the muslin using pins to hold the work at the back of the card. The pins can be adjusted as you place the work squarely onto the card. The fabric should be slightly stretched over the card to prevent wrinkles and folds.

The work now has to be laced together across the back of the work by means of strong thread. Start at the centre of the width of the work. Thread a long length of strong thread onto a tapestry needle and secure at the centre of one of the sides of hemmed edge. Take it over to the other side at the centre and catch at the edge by passing the needle through just once. Return to the first side and repeat 1in (2.5cm) further up the side. Repeat this process until the top of the card has been reached. Leave the thread loose. Repeat this process for the lower half of the sampler, and then again for the length of the sampler. The ends of the thread are now gently tightened until there is no slack, and fastened off. Any pins used to hold the work in place at the back of the work can now be removed. Your work should be sitting square on the card, ready for framing.

It is always wise to choose a professional framer who is familiar with the framing of textiles. Your work should be delivered to the framers ready mounted onto muslin and card. The most important consideration is that the glass should not touch the embroidery. The type of frame should be chosen carefully and most framers will be able to advise you on this. The Royal

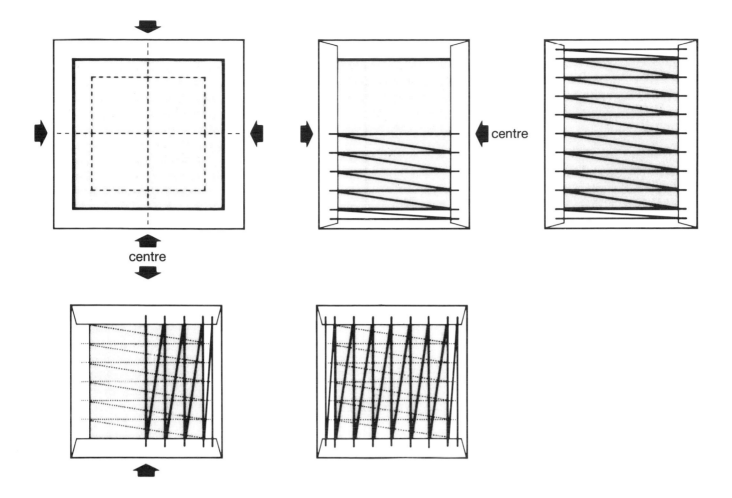

Fig 5   Mounting embroidery onto card

School of Needlework provides a service for mounting embroideries ready for framing and also undertakes cleaning and restoration work. The School can also advise you on the choice of picture framers. I have used Terry Burns Picture Framers at the Royal Academy of Arts in London, who are experienced in this kind of work.

Cleaning and Restoration

Samplers and other types of embroidery should never be placed in direct sunlight or under strong artificial lights. They should also be kept out of direct heat from radiators and fires; the dry atmosphere, fumes and dust particles will, over time, cause irreparable damage, even when the work is framed and behind glass.

Modern samplers can be washed if the fabric and threads that have been used are known to be colour-fast. Use a mild liquid detergent in lukewarm water. Do not wring or squeeze the article; just moving it about gently in the water will be sufficient, but do not leave it to soak. Make sure that it has been thoroughly rinsed before laying it out to dry flat on a white towel (do not dry over a radiator). Pressing should be avoided but should you feel this is necessary, take care

to press only the unworked ground around the stitching.

I do not advise any method of cleaning for old textiles or those that have threads which are not colour-fast; instead, I refer the reader to the following publications:

Finch, K., and Putnam, G., *Caring for Textiles* (Barrie and Jenkins, 1977)
Mailand, H.F., *Consideration for the Care of Textiles and Costumes* (Indianapolis Museum of Art, 1978)
Leene, J.E., *Textile Conservation* (Butterworth, 1972)

There are a small number of firms specialising in the cleaning and restoration of textiles including the Royal School of Needlework, who will undertake work of this kind. Museums with large collections of textiles are also willing to give advice on this subject and the Victoria and Albert Museum in London will advise and help with the dating and identification of older individual pieces of needlework.

5
Stitches

In the following section I have described all the stitches used for the projects in this book. When working the different projects, follow the instructions on the stitches used for the number of threads to be worked over, etc. Some of the stitches I have used are also known by different names, so it would be wise to read through these instructions first before embarking on a project, to avoid confusion.

Plain Cross Stitch
Plain cross stitch consists of two diagonal strokes. The first stroke of each stitch must always be worked in the same direction. When a line or group of stitches are to be worked, I find it best to work the first stroke of all the stitches across one row and then to return back along the row, working the second stroke of the stitches. The next row of stitches is then worked. The work will be neater if the needle is brought up through unworked ground to the right side of the work and down again to the back of the work through a hole shared with a stitch already worked.

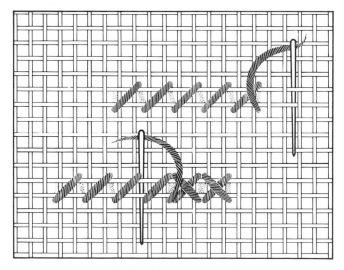

Fig 6   Plain cross stitch

Long-armed Cross Stitch
This is just one variation of cross stitch and is worked in a continuous line or row. It consists of two diagonal strokes; the first is the same as for plain cross stitch but the second return stroke is longer.

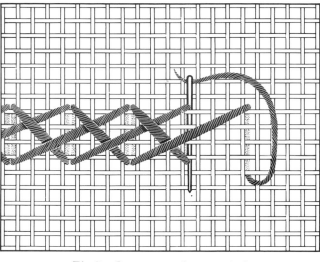

Fig 7   Long-armed cross stitch

Satin Stitch
This is a straight stitch and can be worked vertically, horizontally or diagonally. It is usually worked into every hole and over a number of threads, so covering the fabric well. This is not always the case, and the charts show exactly where the stitches are worked and over how many threads.

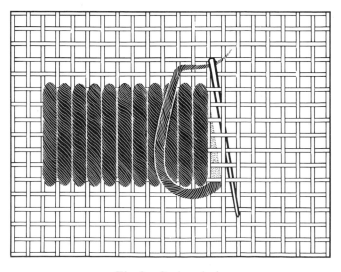

Fig 8   Satin stitch

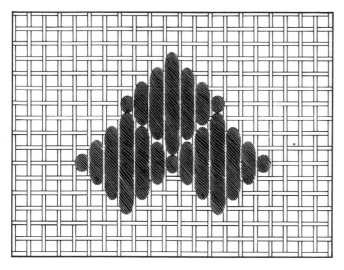

Fig 9   Satin stitch arranged in diamonds

Satin stitch is also used to form different geometric patterns such as triangles and diamonds and herringbone (figs 9-11) which can be used as borders or all-over patterns.

Satin Stitch Trailing

This is satin stitch worked as described above, but over a length of thread or number of threads, which gives a slightly raised, padded effect.

Algerian Eye

This is a stitch using eight or sixteen strokes which occupy a square and radiate from a centre hole. The thread should be pulled through the fabric with a certain degree of tension, so that the centre hole is visible when the stitch is finished; but take care not to distort the shape of the square. Algerian eye is often outlined with back stitch (fig 14).

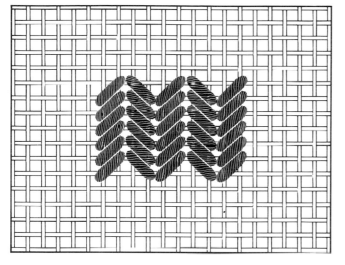

Fig 10   Satin stitch arranged in a chevron pattern

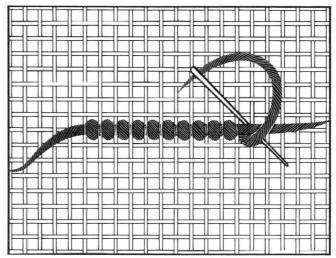

Fig 12   Satin stitch trailing

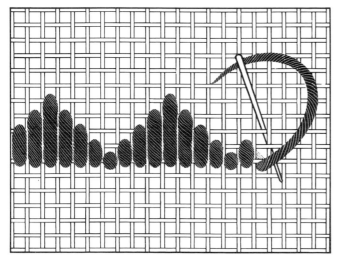

Fig 11   Satin stitch arranged in triangles

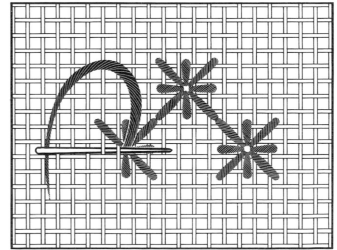

Fig 13   Algerian eye, worked over four by four threads

Fig 14   Algerian eye, worked over eight by eight threads outlined with back stitch.

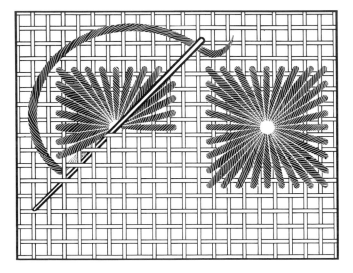

Fig 15   Eyelet worked over eight by eight threads

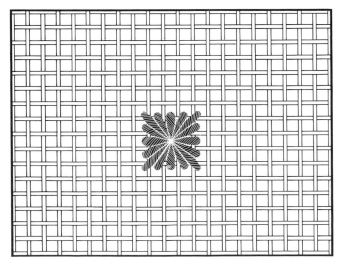

Fig 16   Eyelet worked over four by four threads

Fig 17   One-quarter eyelet worked over four by four threads (top) and five by five threads (bottom)

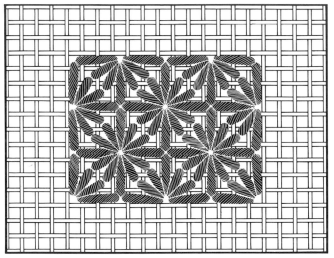

Fig 18   Diamond eyelet

Eyelet

This is very similar to Algerian eye, but there are twice as many strokes so that the finished eyelet has a more solid appearance. One quarter of an eyelet can be used on its own or repeated to form an all-over pattern (see fig 17). It can also be used as a 'diamond' eyelet (fig 18).

Tent (Brick or Continental) Stitch

I have used this stitch for the lettering on many of the samplers in this book and for a few of the motifs. It consists of a diagonal stroke which is always worked in the same direction. On the right side of the work it covers just one thread of the fabric and is worked diagonally. On the wrong side of the embroidery it is worked over at least two threads of the fabric and diagonally.

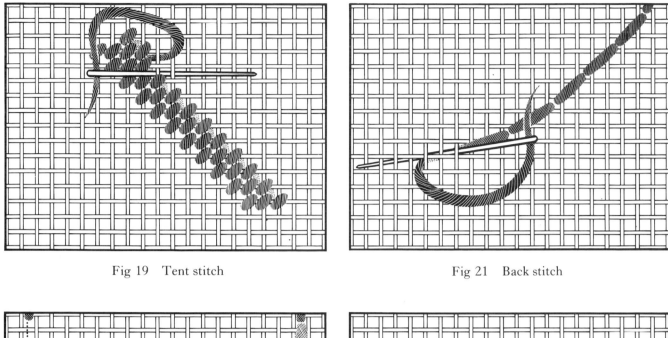

Fig 19   Tent stitch

Fig 21   Back stitch

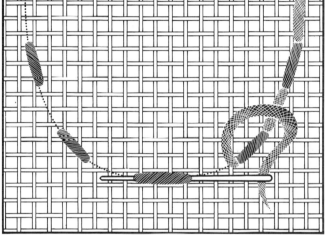

Fig 20   Double running stitch

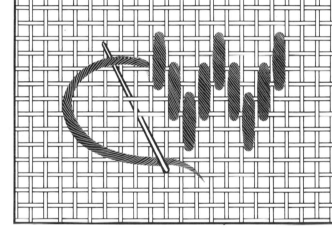

Fig 22   Florentine stitch

When tent stitch is used for lettering a little forethought is required in order to start and end at a place where the strokes of the stitch can be worked as described above. The reverse stroke of the stitch must be worked diagonally and over more than one thread of the fabric.

Double Running Stitch

This is the stitch popularly used for blackwork. It is composed by working straight stitches with spaces between them in one direction and then completing the missing stitches on the way back. This stitch is usually used to outline patterns and designs. Should you find double running stitch difficult to work on a complicated design, you can use back stitch instead.

Back Stitch

This is also a straight stitch and is worked with one stroke on the right side of the fabric.

Florentine Stitch

Florentine is a pattern of straight stitches which can be of the same or varying lengths, using a number of colours. Innumerable different patterns are possible. Tent and cross are a few of the other stitches which are used to create Florentine patterns, but the stitch shown in fig 22 is the stitch referred to as Florentine stitch for the projects in this book.

French Knots

These are made by wrapping the thread around the needle twice, very close to the fabric. The thread is then gently pulled against the needle until it is taut, and the needle is inserted into the fabric two holes from where it emerged; it is then pulled through both the loops on the needle and the fabric.

I have used French knots scattered around the border of the Wedding Celebration sampler (8). They can be used close together to fill an area, producing a textured surface. The thicker the thread, the larger the knot; in counted-thread work, the knots will often need to be worked in thread thicker than that used for the other stitches.

Square Stitch

This uses straight stitches to surround a square. The thread should be pulled fairly firmly on each stroke so that the threads of the fabric are pulled together and the finished stitches form an open, lacy effect.

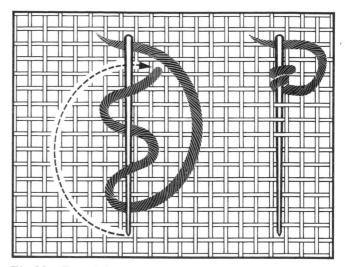

Fig 23   French knot

Fig 24   Square stitch

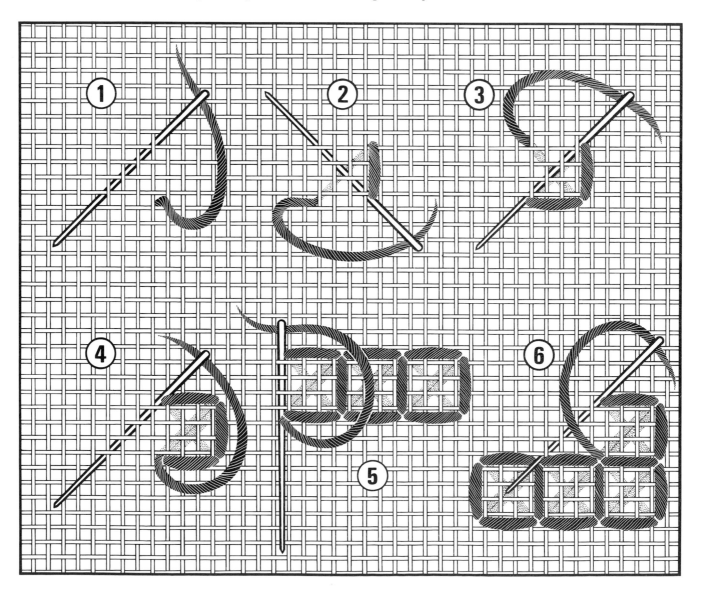

Projects

1
Celebration of a Child's Birthday

(colour photograph page 25)

This design has been worked from a sampler in the Tunbridge Wells Museum in Kent, England. I have worked it in stranded cottons on cream-coloured hardanger fabric, in colours close to the original. There are two cherubs blowing trumpets, two birds and a rather crudely designed but charming pot of flowers in the centre. If the name you wish to include at the bottom is rather longer than the one shown, the surname could be omitted, or the border could be lengthened by working two more whole repeats of the patterns to allow for another line of text underneath.

Fabric
Cream-coloured hardanger fabric, sixteen pairs of threads to 1in (2.5cm). The finished work measures 5½ × 8in (14 × 20cm). When buying your fabric, allow an extra 8in (20cm) on every side.

Thread
Anchor Mouline Stranded Cotton.

Stitch (see Chapter 5)
Cross stitch throughout; three strands are worked over one pair of threads. Each symbol on the chart represents one cross stitch worked in the colour indicated by the colour key.

Colour Key
O	red	042	× 1 skein
X	pink	038	× 1 skein
●	pink	066	× 1 skein
Z	green	0214	× 1 skein
C	beige	0347	× 1 skein
/	brown	360	× 1 skein
•	blue	0850	× 1 skein

All amounts are approximate.

Alphabets and Numerals
Complete sets of the alphabets and numerals are given after the projects. See Alphabet 5 and Numerals 3.

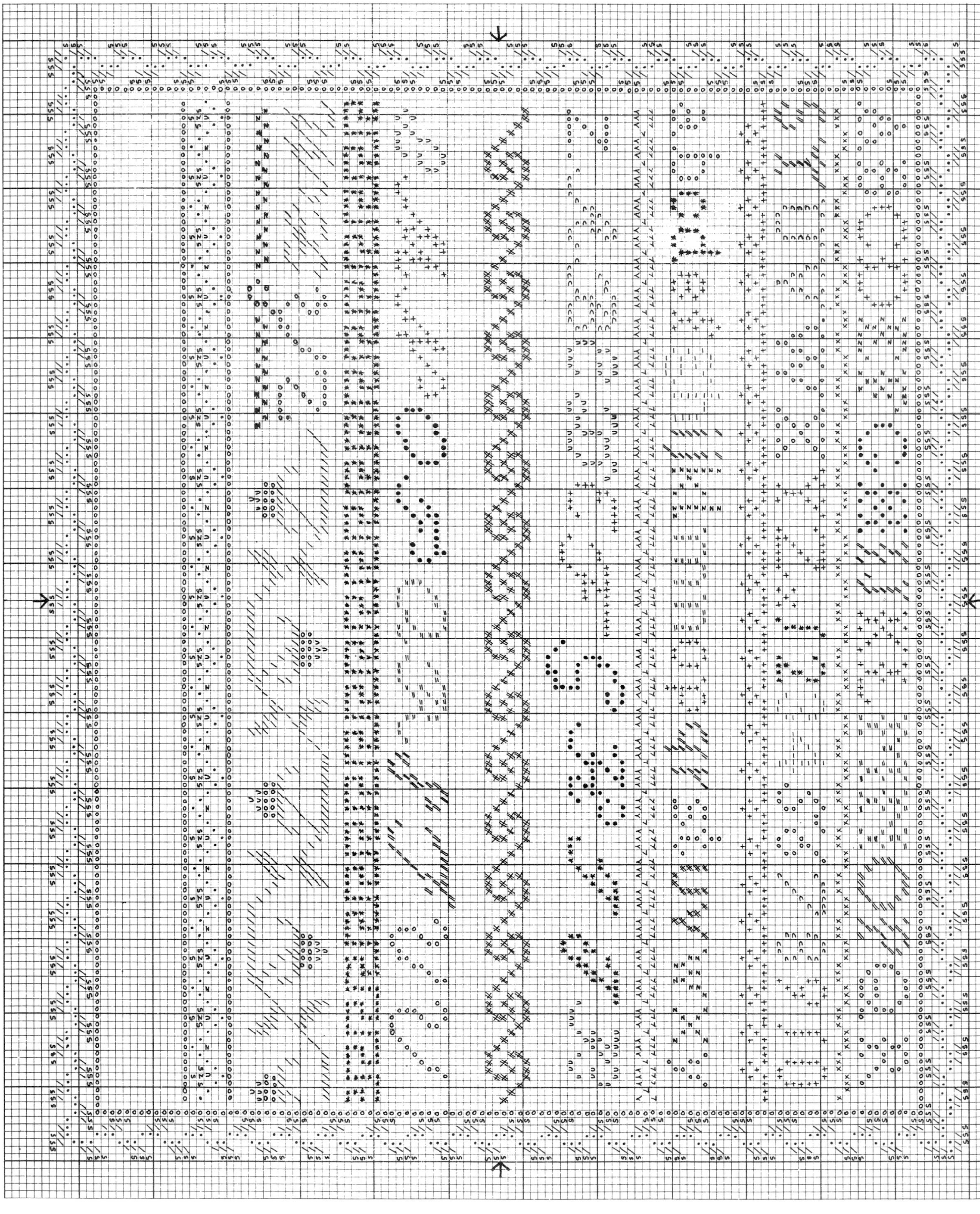

2
Multicoloured Alphabets in Wool

(colour photograph page 26)

This design was inspired by a sampler in the collection of Mrs Pamela Morgan. Her sampler was worked in wool on canvas using many different colours, and is signed 'Ethel Minnie Sedgewick aged 8 years'. The original measures 11 × 15in (28 × 38cm). I have kept the design and colours of this sampler very close to the original, changing a few of the colours which on the original have faded badly, and tidying up some of the border patterns. I have worked the name and date of birth of my son, but you could work your own name and the date on which you completed the sampler. This is a good sampler for beginners to work, as it is simple and uncomplicated but the result is quite charming. Try working it in different colours of your own choice, perhaps using up oddments.

Fabric
Dark-coloured, double-mesh canvas, ten pairs of threads to 1in (2.5cm). The finished work measures 12½ × 15½in (30.5 × 39cm). When buying your fabric, allow an extra 8in (20cm) on every side.

Thread
Coats Tapisserie Wool.

Stitch (see Chapter 5)
Cross stitch throughout, worked over one pair of threads. Each symbol on the chart represents one cross stitch worked in the colour indicated by the colour key.

Colour Key

Symbol	Colour	Code	Amount
O	red	045	× 2 skeins
//	blue	0506	× 1 skein
=	pink	068	× 1 skein
+	grey	0398	× 1 skein
Z	yellow	0734	× 1 skein
C	olive	0268	× 1 skein
✳	brown	0418	× 1 skein
—	purple	0869	× 1 skein
•	green	0269	× 1 skein
/	green	0266	× 1 skein
S	green	0842	× 1 skein
X	green	0215	× 1 skein
>	green	0858	× 1 skein
V	green	0506	× 1 skein
✗	pink	0661	× 1 skein
●	rust	0351	× 1 skein
∧	pink	0895	× 1 skein

All amounts are approximate.

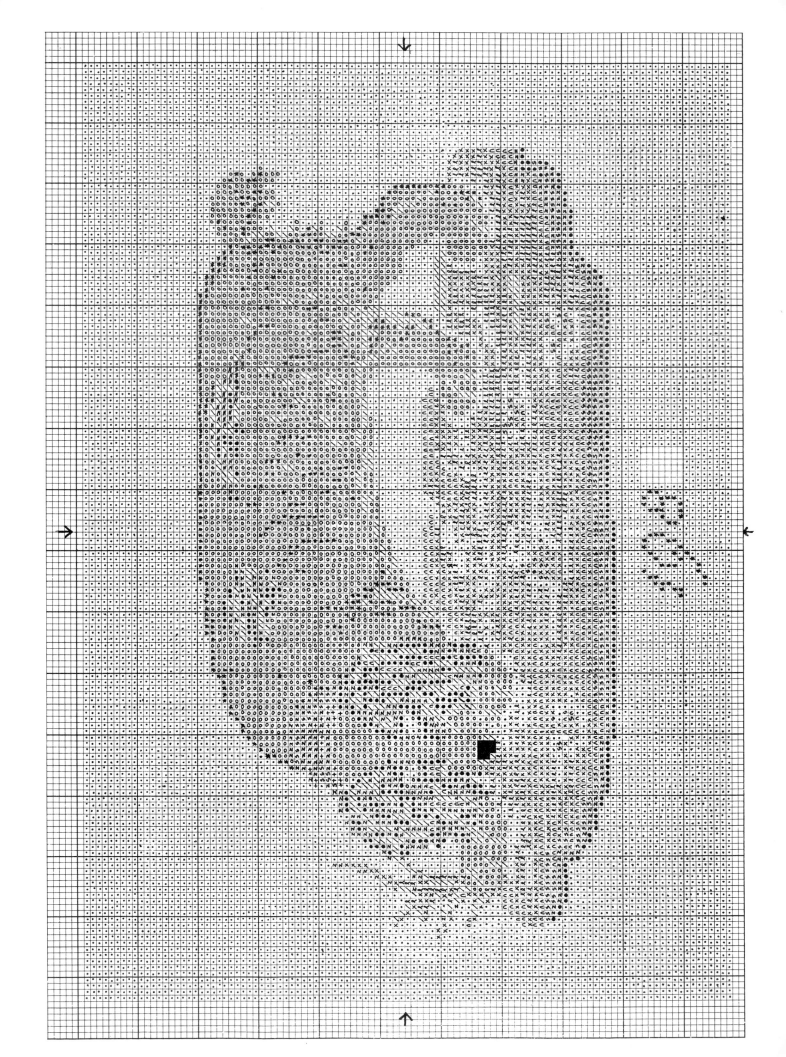

3
Spaniel

(colour photograph page 26)

This design has been taken from a sampler owned by Mr and Mrs Goodwin which is in wool on good-quality sacking! It was worked by a ship's carpenter, H. Baldwin, around 1900. As with all the pieces I have been able to study closely, the original colours have faded, some much more so than others. They were originally very bright and gaudy, but now, with time, they have turned into lovely muted shades, adding much charm and character to the work. I have kept the colours close to those of the original as it appears now. The sampler is worked in wool on double canvas using tent stitch. I have included the year in which it was worked; you could also include your name or initials, using an alphabet from those given.

Fabric
Double-mesh canvas, twelve double threads to 1in (2.5cm). The finished sampler measures 13 × 9in (33 × 23cm). When buying your fabric, allow an extra 8in (20cm) on every side.

Thread
Coats Tapisserie Wool.

Stitch (see Chapter 5)
Tent stitch throughout, worked over one double thread. Each symbol on the chart represents one tent stitch worked in the colour indicated by the colour key.

Colour Key
✱	rust	0741	× 1 skein
+	pink	3166	× 1 skein
Z	beige	0904	× 1 skein
●	brown	0420	× 1 skein
/	sand	0713	× 1 skein
X	green	0859	× 1 skein
ℓ	olive	0269	× 1 skein
•	black	0403	× 4 skcins
∩	brown	0378	× 1 skein
O	white	0390	× 2 skeins
■	pink	0503	× 1 skein
S	cream	0388	× 1 skein

All amounts are approximate.

Numerals
Numerals 12.

4

Adam and Eve

(colour photograph page 27)

This is a Dutch version of Adam and Eve, which I have surrounded with a delicate border of carnations taken from a small hold-all in the Victoria and Albert Museum, London. The hold-all was made in the mid-eighteenth century using silks on linen in cross stitch. I have used the colours from this hold-all, which are rather muted but very pretty. Adam and Eve stand holding hands under the Tree of Knowledge, which is laden with apples. The serpent is also included, along with two rather over-sized birds!

Fabric
Beige evenweave fabric, 27 holes to 1in (2.5cm). The finished sampler measures 8¾ × 10½in (22 × 26.5cm). When buying your fabric, allow an extra 8in (20cm) on every side.

Thread
Coats Coton à Broder.

Stitches (see Chapter 5)
Satin stitch trailing for the lines making the square frame; the thread is used whole over two threads of the fabric and stitched over one whole thread.
All remaining symbols represent cross stitch in the colour indicated by the key; use the thread whole over two threads.

Colour Key
X   green   0260 × 2 skeins
/   pink   8960 × 2 skeins
O   red   0340 × 1 skein
●   blue   0128 × 1 skein
◢   yellow   0298 × 1 skein

All amounts are approximate.

Alphabet
Alphabet 11.

5

Red and Green Alphabets

(colour photograph page 27)

These alphabets and border patterns appear on an American sampler sewn by Elizabeth Lawson and dated 1833. It also shows a number of names and initials, including 'Alexander Thompson American Consul' underneath the American Eagle. I have rearranged some of the alphabets and border patterns into a smaller design using simple basic stitches in the hope that it will appeal to beginners. The first alphabet is in cross stitch, the second is in back stitch and one of the lines of simple border patterns is in eyelets. Colours of your own choice can be substituted for those used here; you could put together any odds and ends you may have to make a large range of colours.

Fabric
White linen evenweave, 26 holes to 1in (2.5cm). The finished sampler measures 7 × 9¼in (17.5 × 23.5cm). When buying your fabric, allow an extra 8in (20cm) on all sides.

Thread
Anchor Mouline Stranded Cotton.

Stitches (see Chapter 5)
Back stitch indicated by solid line; two strands are worked over two threads. This is used for the second alphabet; refer to photograph for colours.
Eyelet (indicated by large star symbol); two strands are worked. The finished eyelet occupies a square of four by four threads. This is used in red for the decoration under the sixth row of letters.
All remaining symbols represent cross stitch in the colour indicated by the key; three strands worked over two threads.

Colour Key
X	red	0341	× 1 skein
•	pink	0339	× 1 skein
O	olive	0856	× 1 skein
/	green	0924	× 1 skein

All amounts are approximate.

Alphabet and Numerals
Alphabet 6, Numerals 7.

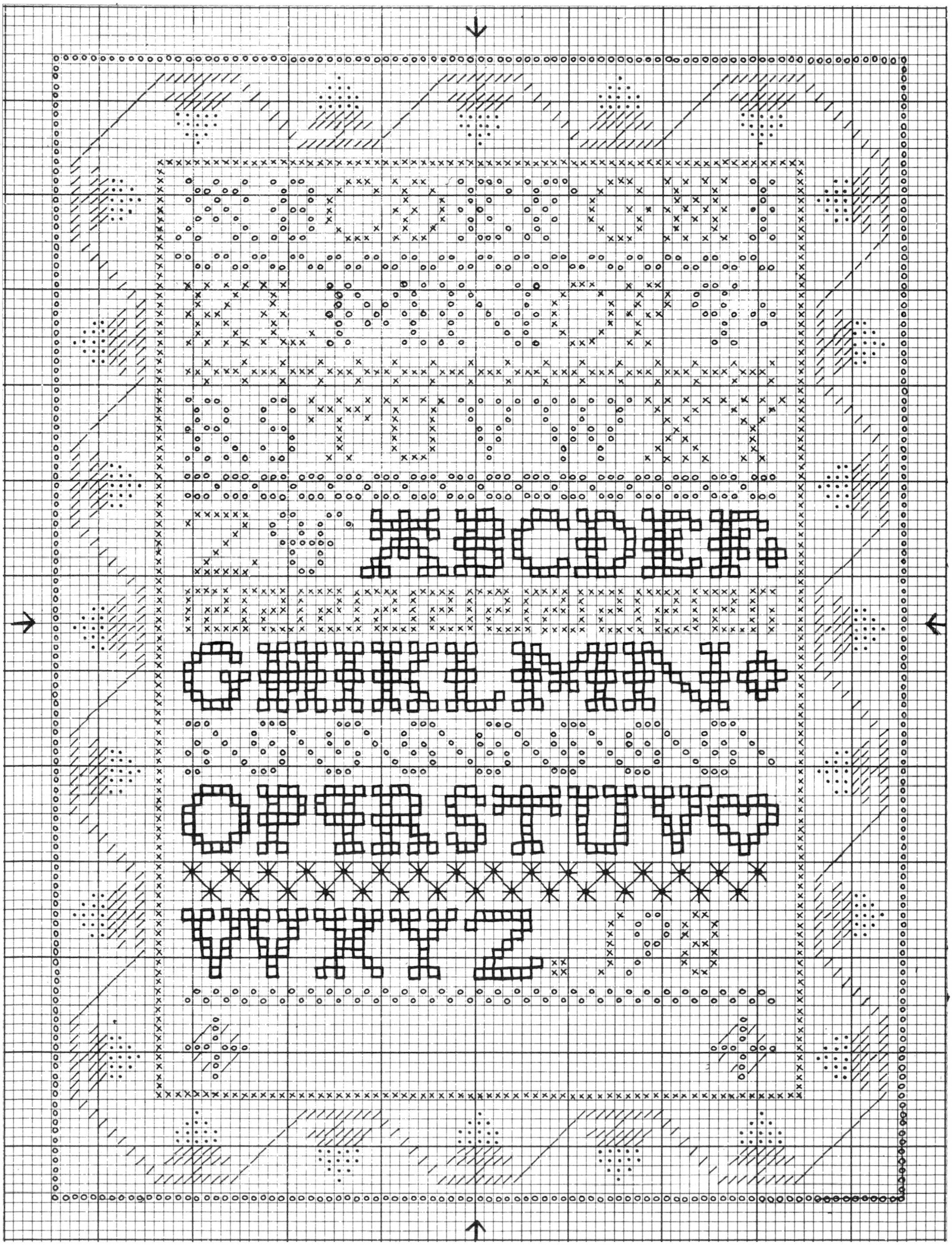

6
American Fort and Animals

(colour photograph page 28, chart pages 72-3)

The designs used for this sampler have been taken from a lovely American sampler worked by nine-year-old Sophia Ellis; it is dated 8 February 1785. She used a large number of religious and secular motifs worked in cross and satin stitches. There are also two alphabets and a set of numerals, together with the words, 'health is a jewel dropped from heaven which money cannot buy the life of . . . peace and pleasant harmony'.

I have included a number of the motifs and designs from the original and worked the sampler in colours as true as possible to those used by Sophia Ellis. The year in which the work is completed is included; you could include your name or an inscription — choose an alphabet from those shown.

Fabric

White evenweave linen, 26 holes to 1in (2.5cm). The finished sampler measures 12½ × 13in (31.5 × 33cm). When buying your fabric, allow an extra 8in (20cm) on every side.

Thread

Anchor Mouline Stranded Cotton; DMC Fil Or (gold thread).

Stitches (see Chapter 5)

Areas of satin stitch are shown by solid lines; three strands of cotton are worked over the number of threads indicated on the chart. Gold thread is used doubled. Refer to photograph for colours.

Back stitch is shown by broken lines; two strands of cotton are worked in black over two threads. Areas within the broken lines to be filled in with satin stitch; refer to photograph for colours.

Satin stitch trailing indicated by thick solid line; three strands of cotton are worked into every hole, over two threads, and stitched over a three-strand length of cotton. This is used for the top row only, in grey.

All remaining symbols represent cross stitch in the colour indicated by the key; two strands worked over two threads. Gold thread is used doubled over two threads.

Colour Key

Anchor Mouline Stranded Cotton:

V	blue	0167 × 2 skeins
O	green	0216 × 2 skeins
●	green	0218 × 2 skeins
•	pink	06 × 1 skein
Z	yellow	0311 × 1 skein (fort, satin stitch)
∩	pink	0895 × 1 skein
S	grey	975 × 1 skein
/	red	0896 × 1 skein
X	black	0403 × 1 skein
✳	DMC Fil Or (gold thread) × 2 reels	

All amounts are approximate.

Numerals

Numerals 3.

7
Red Alphabets

(colour photograph page 27, chart pages 74-5)

This sampler has been put together using alphabets from old pattern books in my collection, which I believe to have been printed in Germany. The alphabet at the top is worked in two shades of red and the second is in script. Underneath I have included the words:

> Sarah Don is my name
> And with my needle
> I wrought the same.

The stitches used for this sampler are very fine and it would not be an easy project for a beginner to work. I have seen a similar piece made up into a small cushion edged with a wide frill of lace, which was very effective.

Fabric
White linen evenweave, 26 holes to 1in (2.5cm). The finished sampler measures 9 × 6¼in (23 × 15.5cm). When buying your fabric, allow an extra 8in (20cm) on every side.

Thread
Coats Coton à Broder

Stitch (see Chapter 5)
Tent stitch throughout worked over a single thread, except for the heart which is in back stitch. Each symbol represents one stitch in the colour indicated by the key.

Colour Key
/   red   019 × 1 skein
•   dark red   044 × 1 skein

All amounts are approximate.

Alphabets and Numerals
Alphabets 10 and 11, Numerals 12.

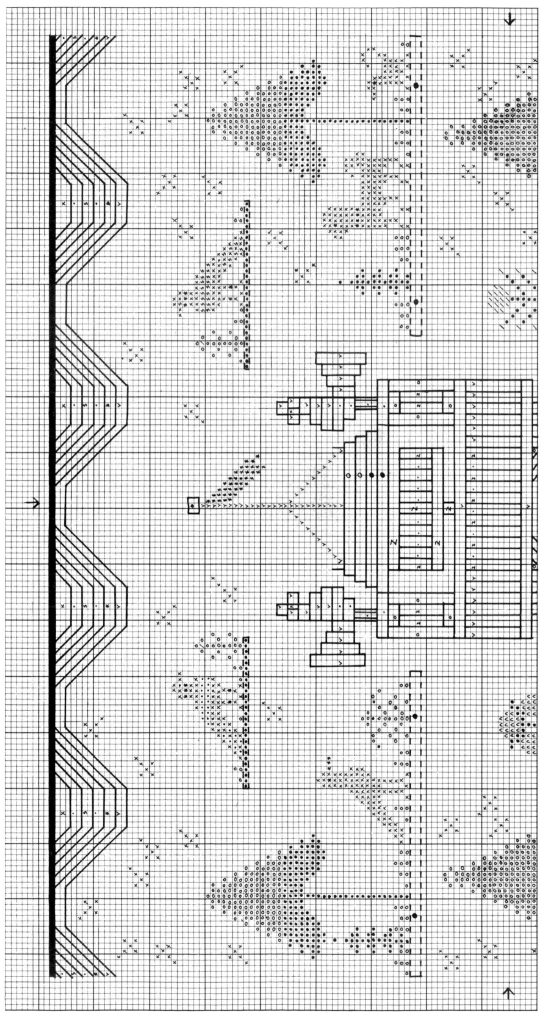

American Fort and Animals

Colour Key

Anchor Mouline Stranded Cotton

V	blue	0167
O	green	0216
●	green	0218
·	pink	06
Z	yellow	0311
∩	pink	0895
S	grey	975
/	red	0896
X	black	0403
✳	DMC Fil Or (gold thread)	

Red Alphabets
Colour Key
/ red
• dark red

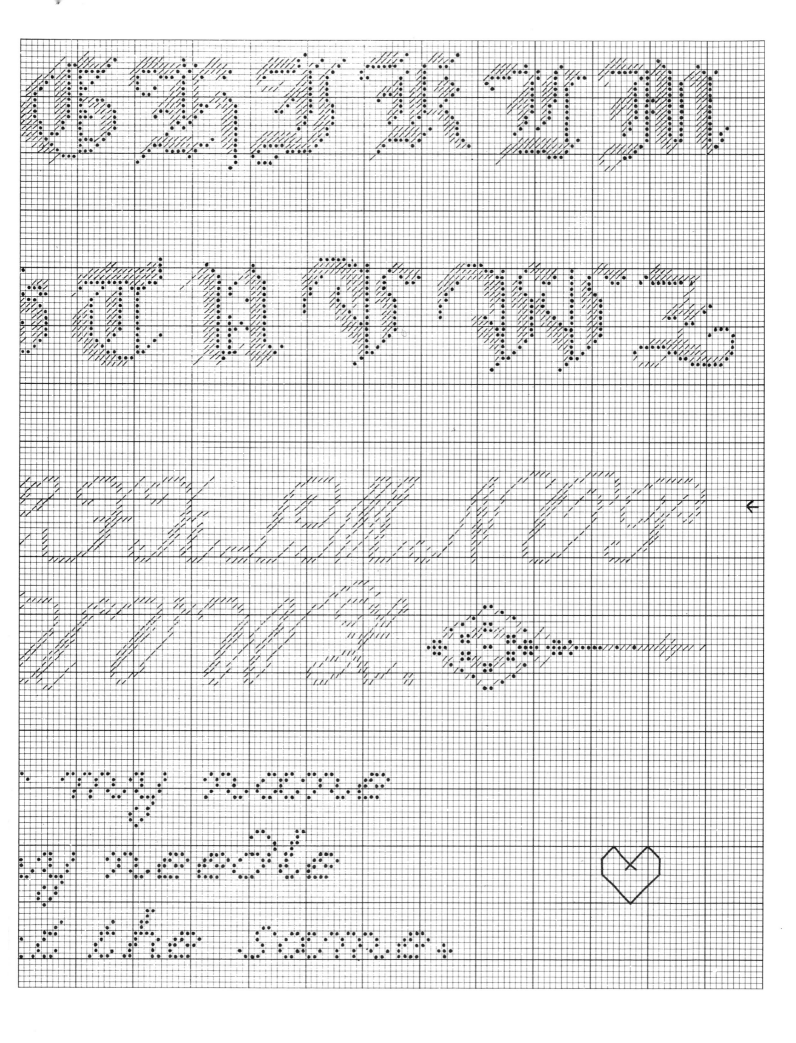

8
Wedding Celebration

(colour photograph page 47, chart pages 78-9)

This sampler is to celebrate a wedding and includes a large amount of text giving details about the couple, their families and the wedding itself. I have used an attractive Dutch alphabet for the text with two cherubs and a heart underneath. This is framed by a Dutch floral border of tulips, roses and carnations, dotted with tiny French knots. I have used the colours which featured in the flowers and the bridesmaids' dresses at the wedding, and have included some silver thread.

For this sampler, you will have to plan the text, making sure that the names and dates are all correct, and then chart carefully the full text into the area for the central section. Remember that each square on the chart represents one stitch and two threads of the fabric. Spaces at the ends of the lines of text can be filled with a motif from those shown with the alphabets. The heart and cherubs can be omitted if you wish to use the whole central space for text.

Fabric
Cream linen evenweave, 28 holes to 1in (2.5cm). The finished sampler measures 13½ × 16½in (34 × 42cm). When buying your fabric, allow an extra 8in (20cm) on every side.

Thread
Anchor Mouline Stranded Cotton.
DMC Fil Argent à Broder (silver thread).

Stitches (see Chapter 5)
Satin stitch for silver triangles; the silver thread is used double (three strands if cotton used).
Satin stitch trailing for straight lines; three strands are worked into every hole over two threads and are stitched over a three-strand length of stranded cotton (see photograph for colours).

French knots; these are worked last, sprinkled around the border in all the colours used, including silver. They are not marked on the chart. The cotton is used with three strands and the silver thread is used double. All remaining symbols represent cross stitch in the colour indicated by the key; two strands worked over two threads.

Colour Key
Anchor Mouline Stranded Cotton:

/	pink	0969	× 1 skein
●	pink	0970	× 1 skein
•	pink	0893	× 1 skein
	purple	0870	× 1 skein (text)
▲	purple	095	× 1 skein
O	purple	0111	× 2 skeins
∩	purple	097	× 1 skein
	purple	096	× 1 skein (text)
	purple	099	× 2 skeins (text)
✳	yellow	0362	× 1 skein
V	brown	0359	× 1 skein
X	green	0861	× 1 skein
Z	orange	010	× 1 skein
	DMC Fil Argent à Broder (silver thread)		

All amounts are approximate.

Alphabets and Numerals
Alphabet 17, Numerals 18.

9
Trees, Flowers and Birds

(colour photograph page 45, chart pages 80-3)

This sampler is based on one in my own collection, which is worked with silks on linen in cross stitch. It bears the words, 'Elizabeth Miles' work Bishop's Lydeard September 1848', and measures 13 × 12in (33 × 30.5cm). The design is perfectly symmetrical, with alphabets, stylised trees, pots of flowers and birds carefully placed around the cloth. It is very typical of samplers from the mid-nineteenth century which were intended to be purely decorative needlework pictures to be hung with pride on the wall.

The design has been copied faithfully from the original but the finished sampler is rather larger. I have included my name, the town I live in and the date on which the sampler was completed.

Fabric

Cream-coloured evenweave fabric, 26 holes to 1in (2.5cm). The finished sampler measures 22½ × 21in (57 × 53cm). When buying your fabric, allow an extra 8in (20cm) on every side.

Thread

Anchor Mouline Stranded Cotton.

Stitch (see Chapter 5)

Cross stitch throughout; two strands are worked over two threads. Each symbol on the chart represents one stitch in the colour indicated by the key.

Colour Key

X	green	0862	× 2 skeins
/	gold	0308	× 2 skeins
O	olive	0846	× 2 skeins
✳	brown	0888	× 2 skeins
●	green	0845	× 1 skein
•	brown	0393	× 1 skein
C	beige	0887	× 1 skein
∩	beige	0373	× 2 skeins
S	brown	0369	× 1 skein

All amounts are approximate.

Wedding celebration

Colour Key
Anchor Mouline Stranded Cotton:

/	pink	0969	◯	purple	0111	V	brown	0359
●	pink	0970	∩	purple	097	X	green	0861
•	pink	0893		purple	096	Z	orange	010
	purple	0870		purple	099		DMC Fil Argent à Broder
▲	purple	095	✳	yellow	0362		(silver thread)

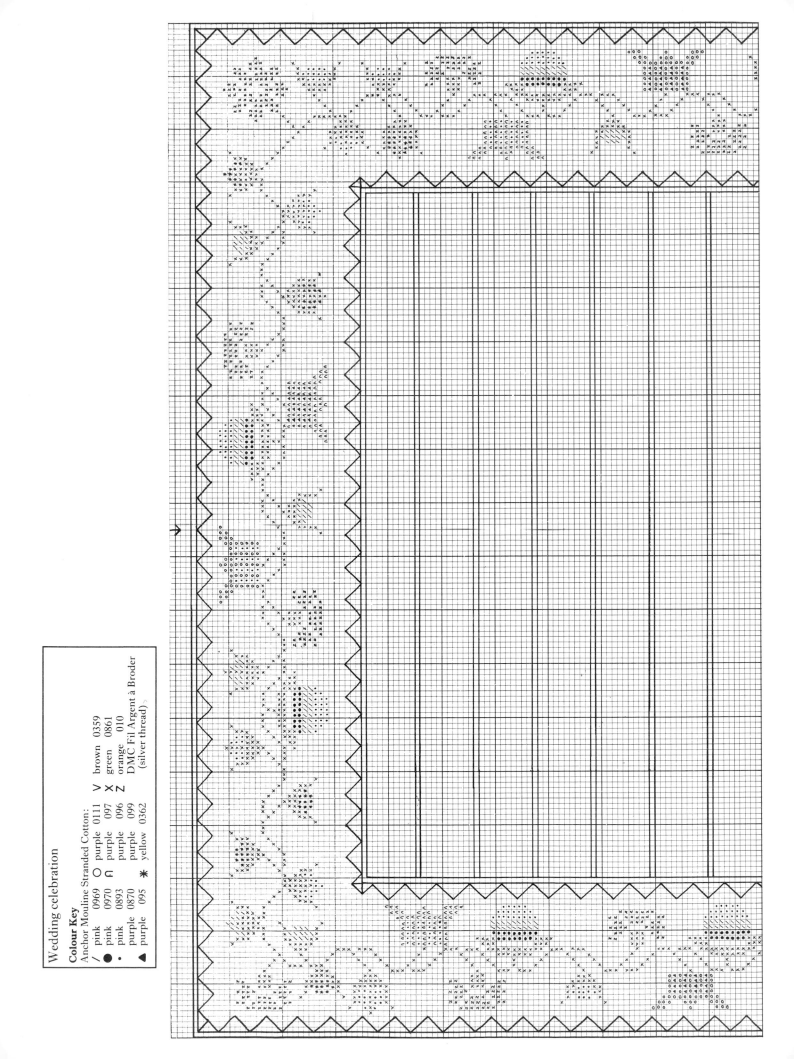

Trees, Flowers and Birds

Colour Key

X	green	0862	●	green	0845
/	gold	0308	•	brown	0393
O	olive	0846	C	beige	0887
✳	brown	0888	∩	beige	0373
			S	brown	0369

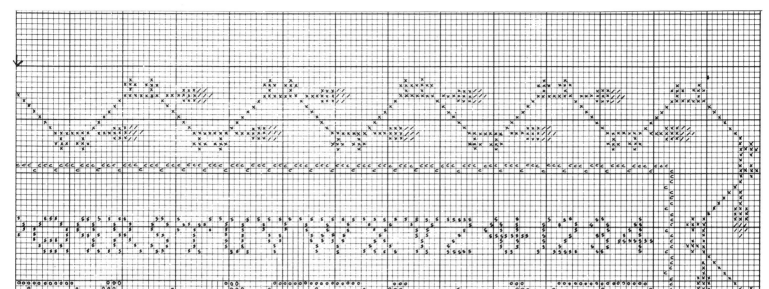

Trees, Flowers and Birds

Colour Key

X	green	0862	● green	0845
/	gold	0308	• brown	0393
O	olive	0846	C beige	0887
✳	brown	0888	∩ beige	0373
S	brown	0369		

83

10
Child Holding a Rabbit

(colour photograph page 48, chart pages 86-7)

This is a design taken from a woolwork sampler in my own collection, which is worked on a light-coloured canvas in wools which are now rather faded. On the original, the child's purple trousers have faded to blue and beige. This is a very pretty though modest sampler, the attempt at shading showing the trend for more realistic designs; the use of colour is typical of this type of sampler from the Victorian period. It was worked by a little girl called Alice Mitchell, aged eight. I have copied the original quite faithfully, although my design works out a little larger.

Fabric
Cream double canvas, nine pairs of threads to 1in (2.5cm). The finished sampler measures 19 × 21in (48 × 53cm). When buying your fabric, allow an extra 8in (20cm) on every side.

Thread
Coats Tapisserie Wool.

Stitch (see Chapter 5)
Cross stitch throughout, worked over one pair of threads. Each symbol represents one stitch in the colour indicated by the key.

Alphabets and Numerals
Alphabets 5 and 6, Numerals 7.

Colour Key

Symbol	Colour	Number	Amount
ℓ	brown	0351	× 1 skein
△	brown	0358	× 1 skein
I	brown	0380	× 1 skein
U	beige	0373	× 1 skein
⊿	stone	0388	× 1 skein
Q	brown	0845	× 1 skein
y	olive	0424	× 1 skein
●	white	0725	× 1 skein
X	blue	0506	× 3 skeins
//	green	0264	× 1 skein
h	pink	0503	× 1 skein
▢	pink	0069	× 1 skein
/	pink	0037	× 3 skeins
꜀	blue	0139	× 1 skein
∞	black	0360	× 1 skein
b	blue	0145	× 1 skein
—	brown	0903	× 1 skein
※	beige	0390	× 1 skein
O	green	0842	× 3 skeins
∩	yellow	3230	× 1 skein
Z and ▲	pink	3098	× 1 skein
S and ∽	grey	0397	× 1 skein
+	white	0441	× 1 skein
✕	grey	0401	× 1 skein
C	purple	099	× 1 skein
L	purple	095	× 1 skein
V	purple	097	× 1 skein
✳	red	045	× 1 skein
.	pink	0336	× 1 skein
t	beige	0570	× 1 skein
ꝯ	brown	0420	× 1 skein

All amounts are approximate.

11
Alphabets and Border Patterns

(colour photograph page 46, chart pages 88-93)

This sampler includes a large number of my favourite alphabets, border patterns and crowns which have been taken from samplers dating from the last four centuries and from around the world. I have tried not to repeat these designs elsewhere in the book and they are meant as a source of patterns for you to use when designing your own samplers. Try experimenting with different colours and stitches. My initials and the year in which I completed the sampler are included.

The first alphabet, which is Dutch, is given rather elaborate treatment. It is worked in cross stitch with a pattern worked in back stitch in a contrasting colour around the edges of the letters. The second alphabet is worked in Algerian eye and the third, worked in cross stitch, came from a German pattern book in my own collection. The border patterns underneath include some old favourites which were popularly used — rosebud, honeysuckle, strawberry, tulip and carnation. The large floral pattern at the bottom is taken from a pattern book by Peter Quentel printed in the sixteenth century. The cartouche containing the date is taken from an English sampler in my own collection, dated 1826; I have seen many versions of this on samplers from England and Holland.

Fabric
Natural Glenshee evenweave linen, 29 holes to 1in (2.5cm). The finished sampler measures 20 × 25in (53 × 71cm). When buying your fabric, allow an extra 8in (20cm) on every side.

Thread
Anchor Mouline Stranded Cotton

Stitches (see Chapter 5)
Back stitch (indicated by broken or solid line with no symbol); two strands are worked over two threads (see photograph for colour).
Algerian eye (indicated by large star symbol); two strands are worked so that the finished stitch occupies a square of four by four threads (see photograph for colour).
Satin stitch (solid line with colour symbol inside); two strands are worked into every hole over the number of threads indicated on the chart.
All remaining symbols represent cross stitch in the colour indicated by the key; two strands worked over two threads.

Colour and Stitch Key

Symbol	Colour	Amount
/	blue	0161 × 2 skeins
∧ and ∨	blue	0851 × 2 skeins
●	red	011 × 2 skeins
✳	olive	0845 × 2 skeins
X	green	216 × 2 skeins
Z	yellow	297 × 2 skeins
O	pink	9 × 2 skeins
----□	back stitch (see photograph for colour)	
✦◇✦	satin stitch (colour indicated by symbols)	
✳	Algerian eye (see photograph for colour)	

All amounts are approximate.

Alphabet and Numerals
Alphabet 11, Numerals 12.

Child Holding a Rabbit

Colour Key

ℓ	brown	0351
$\triangle$	brown	0358
I	brown	0380
U	beige	0373
$\angle$	stone	0388
Q	brown	0845
y	olive	0424
●	white	0725
X	blue	0506
$//$	green	0264
h	pink	0503
$\square$	pink	0069
$/$	pink	0037
6	blue	0139
∞	black	0360
b	blue	0145
$-$	brown	0903
✖	beige	0390
O	green	0842
$\cap$	yellow	3230
Z and ▲	pink	3098
S and $\cup$	grey	0397
$+$	white	0441
✕	grey	0401
C	purple	099
L	purple	095
V	purple	097
✳	red	045
•	pink	0336
t	beige	0570
9	brown	0420

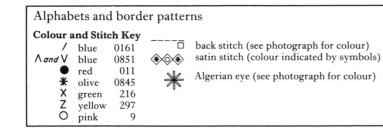

Alphabets and border patterns

Colour and Stitch Key

/	blue	0161
∧ and ∨	blue	0851
●	red	011
✱	olive	0845
X	green	216
Z	yellow	297
O	pink	9

- - - - □	back stitch (see photograph for colour)
✦◇✦	satin stitch (colour indicated by symbols)
✳	Algerian eye (see photograph for colour)

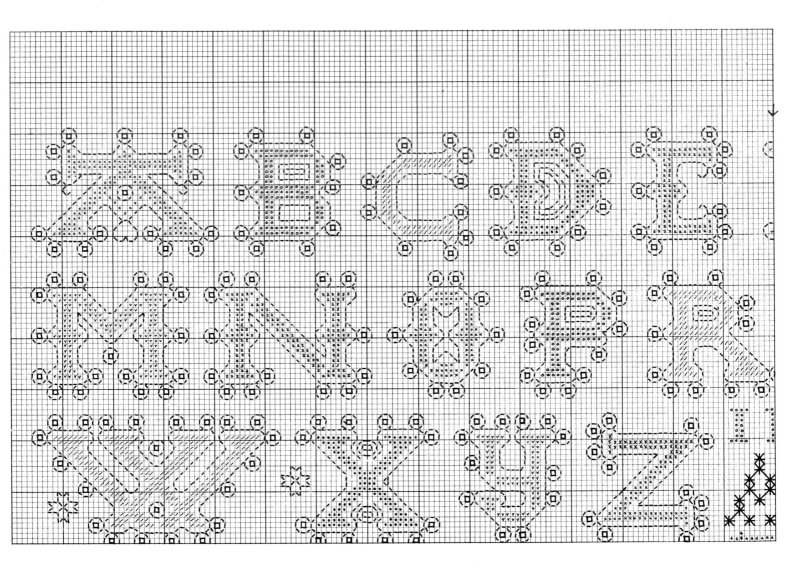

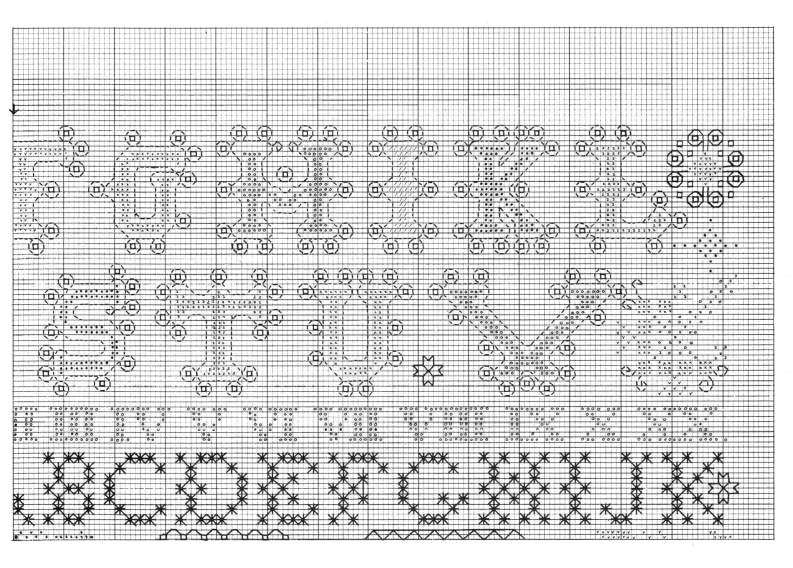

Alphabets and border patterns

Colour and Stitch Key

/	blue	0161
∧ and ∨	blue	0851
●	red	011
✳	olive	0845
X	green	216
Z	yellow	297
O	pink	9

‒ ‒ ‒ ‒ □ back stitch (see photograph for colour)

✦◇✦ satin stitch (colour indicated by symbols)

✳ Algerian eye (see photograph for colour)

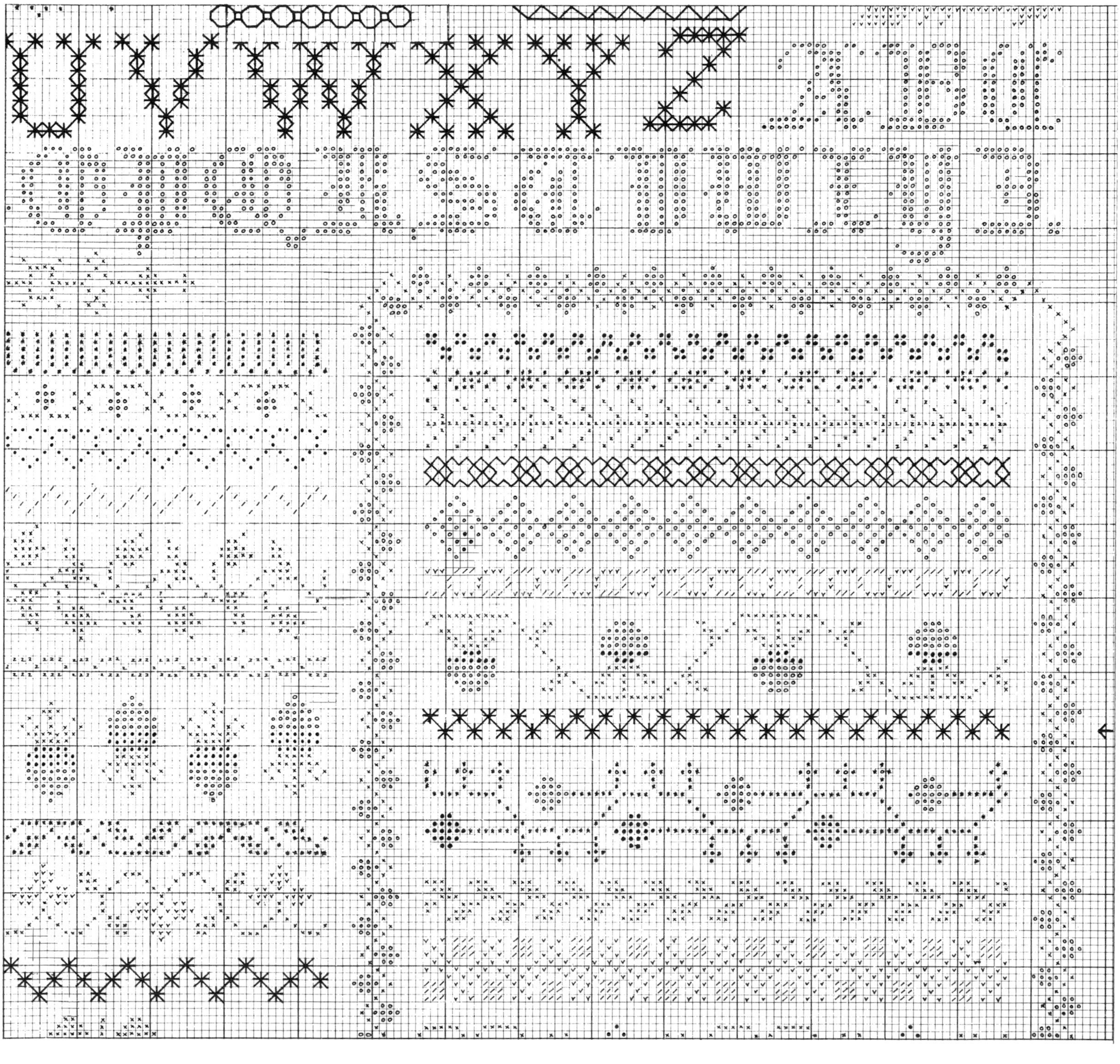

Alphabets and border patterns

Colour and Stitch Key

Symbol	Colour	Number
/	blue	0161
∧ and ∨	blue	0851
●	red	011
✳	olive	0845
X	green	216
Z	yellow	297
O	pink	9

------□ back stitch (see photograph for colour)

✷◇✷ satin stitch (colour indicated by symbols)

✳ Algerian eye (see photograph for colour)

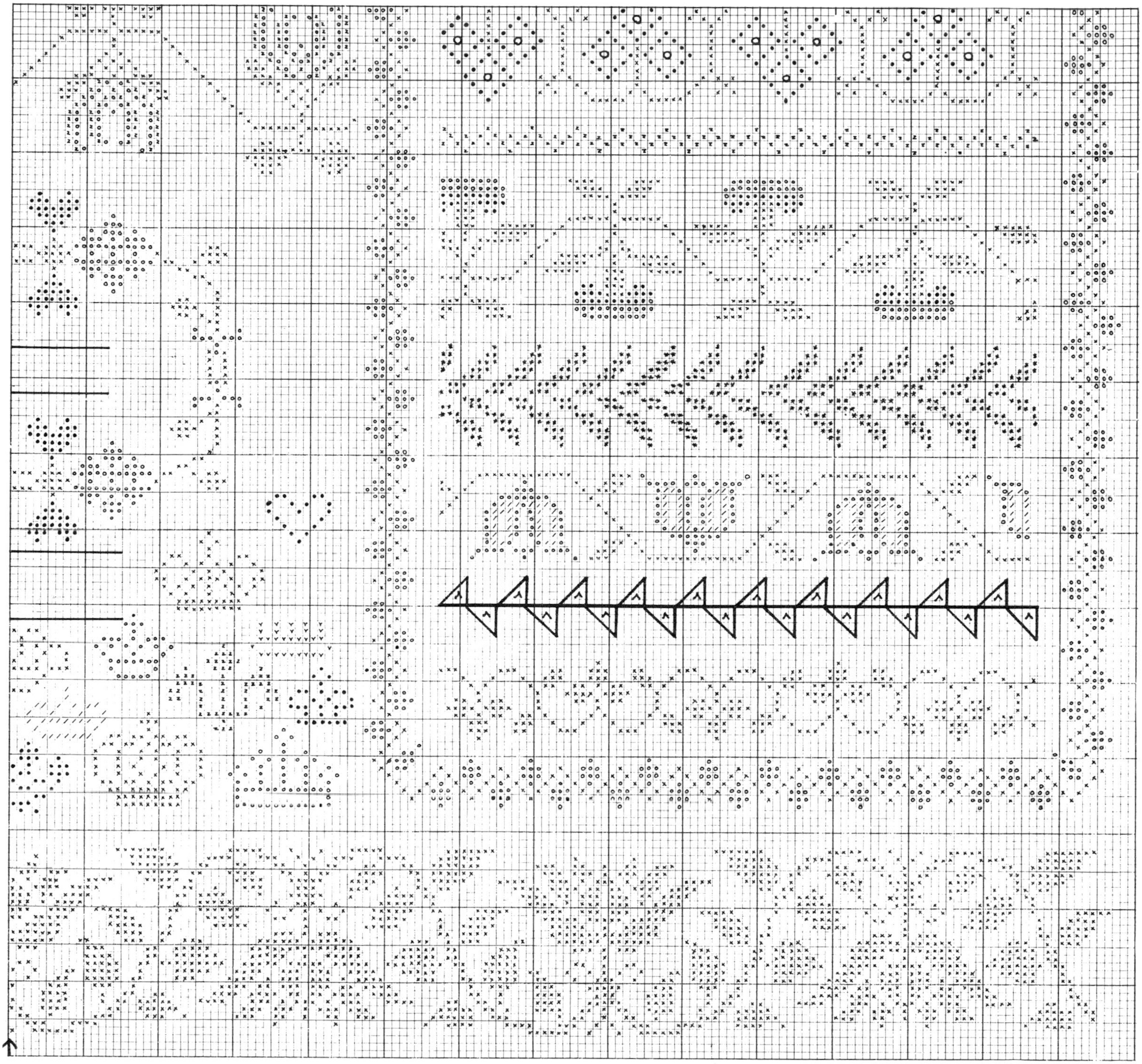

Gift Sampler
Colour Key

•	red	011	/	grey	848	white 0926
○	brown	0905		peach	0347	(satin-stitch wall)
X	brown	0379	Z	pink	0882	= brown 382

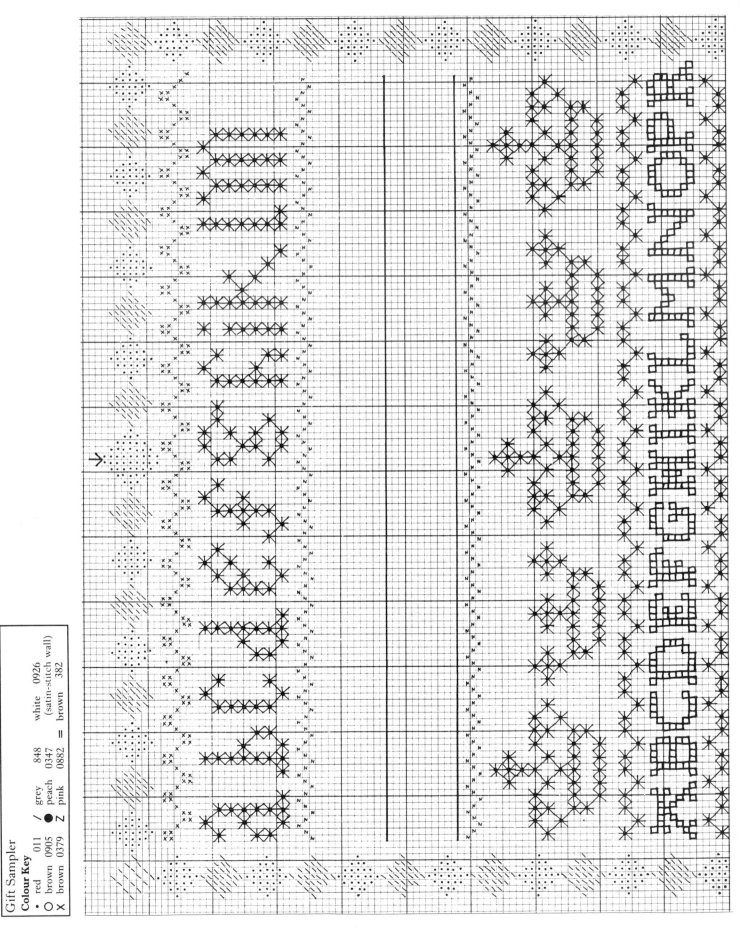

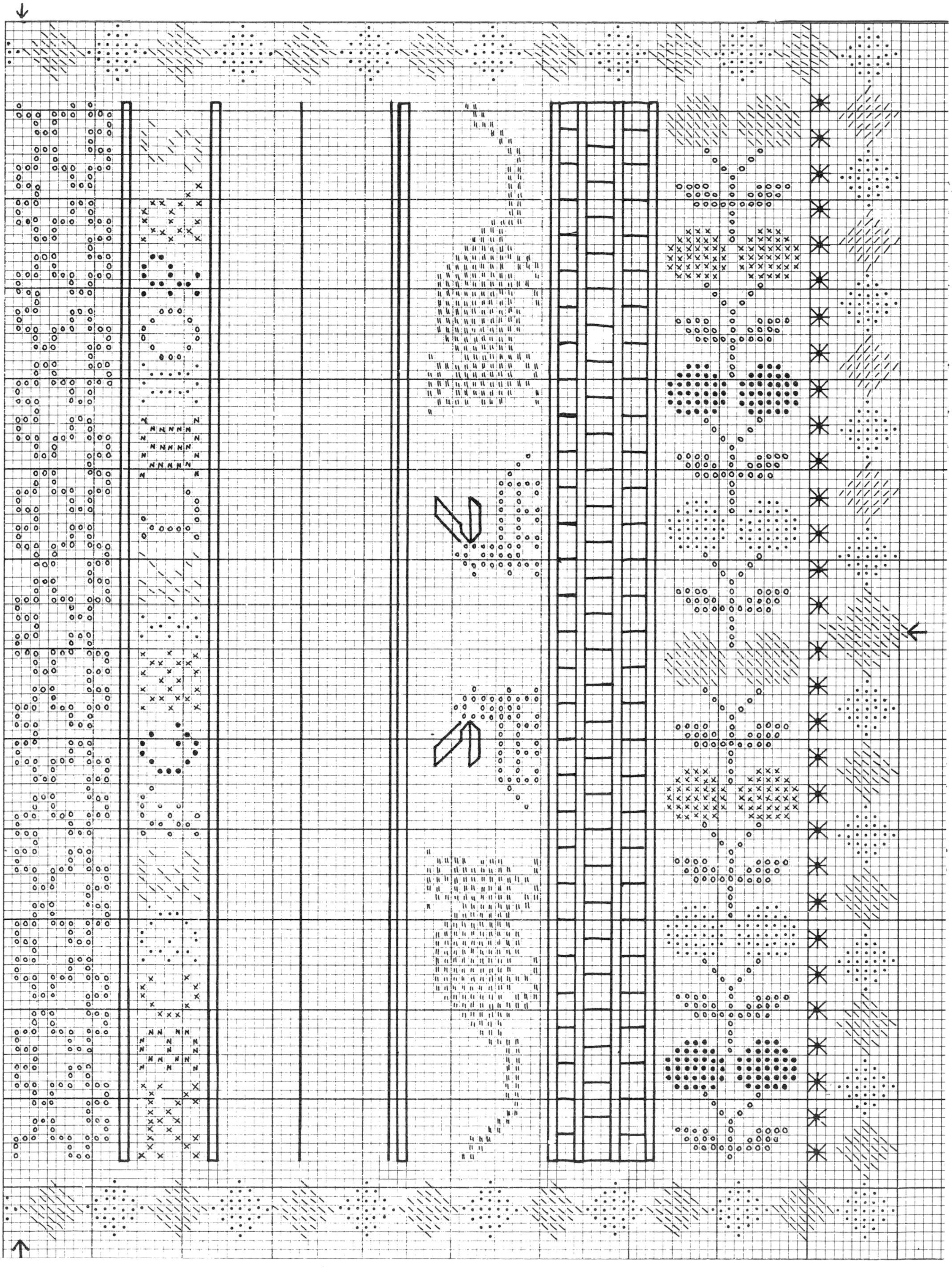

12

Gift Sampler

(colour photograph page 98, chart pages 94-5)

The alphabets used here were taken from an English sampler dated 1733. Border patterns from other English pieces of about the same time have also been incorporated into the design, together with Dutch cats and rabbits. I worked this particular sampler for two young friends of mine who each have a cat and a rabbit as pets. You may like to work a different group of motifs into this area. The different alphabets are worked in eyelet, cross stitch and satin stitch trailing. The brick pattern is worked using satin stitch in between rows of satin stitch trailing. The areas left blank on the charts are for your own text, and there are guidelines to help with positioning (do not stitch lines).

Fabric
Soft cream linen evenweave, 27 holes to 1in (2.5cm). The finished sampler measures 10¼ × 14½in (26 × 37cm). When buying your fabric, allow an extra 8in (20cm) on every side.

Thread
Anchor Mouline Stranded Cotton.

Stitches (see Chapter 5)
Satin stitch for second alphabet and wall; three strands are worked over two threads unless otherwise shown on chart (see photograph for colours).

Eyelet (indicated by large star symbol); three strands are worked over two threads. The completed stitch occupied a square of four by four threads (see photograph for colour).
Satin stitch trailing for horizontal lines; three strands are worked over two threads, over a length of three strands of cotton (see photograph for colours).
Back stitch in black has been used for the rabbit's ears. All remaining symbols represent cross stitch in the colour indicated by the key; three strands worked over two threads.

Colour Key
•	red	011	× 2 skeins
O	brown	0905	× 2 skeins
X	brown	0379	× 1 skein
/	grey	848	× 2 skeins
●	peach	0347	× 1 skein
Z	pink	0882	× 1 skein
	white	0926	× 1 skein (satin-stitch wall)
=	brown	382	× 1 skein

All amounts are approximate.

Alphabets and Numerals
Alphabets 5, 8, 9, 25 and 27, Numerals 26.

(opposite) Multiplication Table (p101); Busy Bee (p108); Valentine (p106)
(overleaf) Gift Sampler (p96); Noah's Ark (p109)

MULTIPLICATION·TABLE·S·DON·⊗

1	2	3	4	5	6	7	8	9	10	11	12
2	4	6	8	10	12	14	16	18	20	22	24
3	6	9	12	15	18	21	24	27	30	33	36
4	8	12	16	20	24	28	32	36	40	44	48
5	10	15	20	25	30	35	40	45	50	55	60
6	12	18	24	30	36	42	48	54	60	66	72
7	14	21	28	35	42	49	56	63	70	77	84
8	16	24	32	40	48	56	64	72	80	88	96
9	18	27	36	45	54	63	72	81	90	99	108
10	20	30	40	50	60	70	80	90	100	110	120
11	22	33	44	55	66	77	88	99	110	121	132
12	24	36	48	60	72	84	96	108	120	132	144

1951.

ABCDEF GHIJKL MNO PQRSTUV
WX YZ abcdef ghijklmn opqrstuvg

How doth the little busy bee
Improve each shining hour
And gather honey all the day
From every opening flower
++++++++++ WXYZ ++++++++

I sewid this for my daughter Ottillie
zian 1985

♥ BERNARD,
♥

1964

a b c d e f g h i k l m n

For Sarah & Steven on ~~~
their 6th birthday 13·3·1985

A B C D E F G H I K L M N O P R

A B C D E F G H K L M N O P R S

here a figure there a letter
one done bad some better

Noah sent forth a 🕊 out

of the 🚢 that

came to him again in the eve

-ning with an olive 🌿 that

she had plucked in her 🕊 so

Noah knew that the Waters

were abated from the earth.

Sarah Don 1985

13
Multiplication Table

(colour photograph page 97, chart pages 102-5)

These tables were often worked by children as popular school exercises, though they were not always correct. I have worked mine with a typically English honeysuckle border and included a Dutch landscaped scene at the bottom. This scene has been worked by English sampler-makers several times, in various degrees of complexity and using different colours. I have also worked two garlands of flowers in which you can work dates or initials. The table could be worked on its own and surrounded just by the border given here or with one of your own choice. (See page 51 for advice on turning the corners of borders.)

Fabric
Cream Danish linen evenweave, thirty holes to 1in (2.5cm). The finished sampler measures 16¼ × 17¼in (41 × 44cm). When buying your fabric, allow an extra 8in (20cm) on every side.

Thread
DMC Stranded Cotton.

Stitch (see Chapter 5)
Cross stitch throughout; two strands are worked over two threads. Each symbol represents one cross stitch in the colour indicated by the key.

Colour Key

Symbol	Colour	Number	Amount
X	blue	926	× 2 skeins
h	red	3350	× 3 skeins
/	blue	930	× 1 skein
C	yellow	743	× 1 skein
✳	red	315	× 2 skeins
V	pink	950	× 1 skein
●	olive	3012	× 2 skeins
O	green	730	× 1 skein
+	pink	407	× 1 skein
t	green	859	× 1 skein
•	brown	938	× 1 skein
S	blue	501	× 1 skein
L	green	956	× 1 skein
Z	brown	379	× 1 skein

All amounts are approximate.

Alphabet
Alphabet 4.

(opposite) Blackwork Sampler (p116)

Multiplication Table

Colour Key
X	blue	926	✳	red	315	t	green	859
h	red	3350	V	pink	950	•	brown	938
/	blue	930	●	olive	3012	S	blue	501
C	yellow	743	O	green	730	L	green	956
			+	pink	407	Z	brown	379

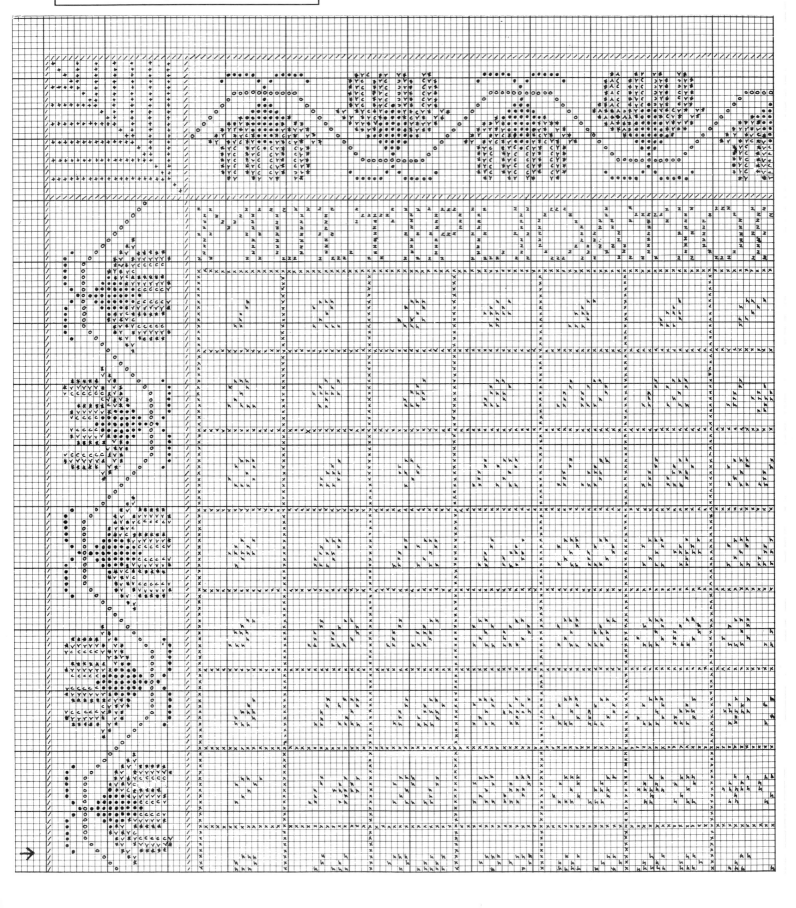

Colour Key

X	blue	926	✳	red	315
h	red	3350	V	pink	950
/	blue	930	●	olive	3012
C	yellow	743	O	green	730
			+	pink	407

t	green	859
•	brown	938
S	blue	501
L	green	956
Z	brown	379

14

Valentine

(colour photograph page 97)

Samplers were often made and given as tokens of affection. This one is similar in style to the Valentines made around the turn of the century, and often exchanged between soldiers and their wives/girlfriends during World War I. The colours are my own choice, although the motifs are traditionally used on samplers. All of them have different symbolic meanings; you could use appropriate motifs of your own choice (see pages 36-7, on symbolism). The lettering has been taken from an old German pattern book.

Fabric
White linen evenweave, 28 holes to 1in (2.5cm). The finished sampler measures 8½ × 4¼in (21.5 × 11cm). When buying your fabric, allow an extra 8in (20cm) on every side.

Thread
Coats Coton à Broder.

Stitches (see Chapter 5)
Motifs C-E and lettering: tent stitch, worked over a single thread.
Motifs A and B: white satin stitch outlined in red back stitch (dotted line), worked over the number of threads shown on the chart.
All remaining symbols represent cross stitch worked over two threads in colours indicated by key.

Colour Key
/	yellow	298	× 1 skein
✱	red	47	× 1 skein
○	green	262	× 1 skein
·	purple	101	× 1 skein (and text)
●	white	396	× 1 skein

Alphabets and Numerals
Alphabets 15, Numerals 16.

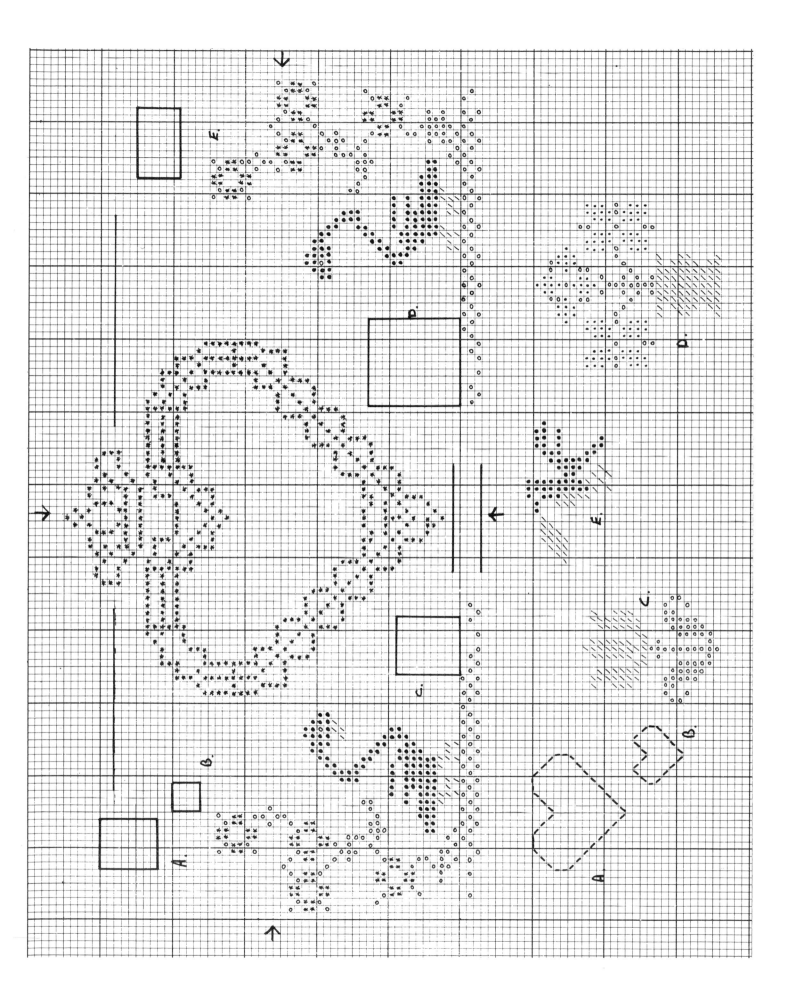

15

Busy Bee

(colour photograph page 97, chart pages 110-11)

This sampler is based on one from the second half of the nineteenth century which bears the name of St Mary's National Girls' School but is not signed or dated. It shows a pretty pink building representing the school, with alphabets, lines of Biblical text, a basket of fruit, flowers and a tree. The whole is surrounded by a strawberry border — a very popular design which appeared time and again without much variation in either style or colour.

The sampler was unfinished; the space around the building was probably meant to be filled with a number of different motifs. I rather like the space fairly empty and have included only a beehive and flowers in the design to complement the poem which I have used to replace the Biblical text. You may wish to fill in the area with some of your favourite motifs. The colours I have used are close to those used in the original. At the bottom there is an inscription dedicating the work to one of my daughters; space permitting, you can substitute the inscription of your choice. The date on which I completed the sampler is worked into the bottom corners of the border, the day and the month in the left-hand corner, the year in the right-hand corner. If there is not enough room for the month in letters, it can be worked in numerals.

Fabric

Off-white linen evenweave, 27 holes to 1in (2.5cm). The finished sampler measures 13¾ × 17½in (35 × 44.5cm). When buying your fabric, allow an extra 8in (20cm) on every side.

Thread

Anchor Mouline Stranded Cotton.

Stitches *(see Chapter 5)*

House: satin stitch (white horizontal and vertical 'frame'); three strands are worked into every hole and over six threads. The rest of the house is in tent stitch; all six strands worked over two threads.

Eyelet (for decoration between alphabets); use three strands of dark blue. The finished eyelet occupies a square of four by four threads.

All remaining symbols represent cross stitch in the colour indicated by key; three strands worked over two threads.

Colour Key

X	green	0878	× 3 skeins
•	red	013	× 3 skeins
●	pink	0895	× 3 skeins
O	pink	6	× 1 skein
/	blue	0145	× 2 skeins
S	blue	158	× 1 skein
✳	yellow	0307	× 1 skein
C	brown	382	× 1 skein
//	white	01	× 3 skeins

All amounts are approximate.

Numerals

Numerals 30.

16
Noah's Ark

(colour photograph page 99, chart pages 112-13)

Rebus samplers such as this were made in the eighteenth century as one of many school needlework exercises; rebuses were, however, rather rare. The story of Noah's ark lends itself well to this kind of treatment, as would many classical stories and nursery rhymes. The words that are missing from the text are replaced by pictures, in this case dove, ark, leaf and beak.

I have used the same text and lettering as in a sampler made in 1793 by ten-year-old Elizabeth Bullocks. The ark, doves and the border are different, and I have included a rising sun at the bottom.

Fabric
White linen evenweave fabric, 26 holes to 1in (2.5cm). The finished sampler measures 12 × 15in (30.5 × 38cm). When buying your fabric, allow an extra 8in (20cm) on every side.

Thread
Anchor Mouline Stranded Cotton.

Stitches (scc Chapter 5)
Areas of satin stitch shown within lines; three strands are worked over the number of threads indicated on the chart (see photograph for colours). Satin stitch is used freehand for leaves and sun's rays.

All remaining symbols represent cross stitch in the colour indicated by the key; three strands worked over two threads.

Colour Key

X	blue	0152	× 2 skeins
C	yellow	311	× 1 skein (satin-stitch sun)
/	green	0267	× 1 skein
✳	green	0269	× 1 skein
O	green	0261	× 1 skcin
•	white	01	× 1 skein
V	rust	5975	× 1 skein (satin-stitch ark)
Z	pink	0892	× 1 skein
●	brown	944	× 1 skein
■	blue	0976	× 2 skeins (satin-stitch sea and border)

All amounts are approximate.

Alphabets and Numerals
Alphabets 20 and 22, Numerals 10.

Busy Bee
Colour Key
X	green	0878
•	red	013
●	pink	0895
○	pink	6
/	blue	0145
S	blue	158
✱	yellow	0307
C	brown	382
//	white	01

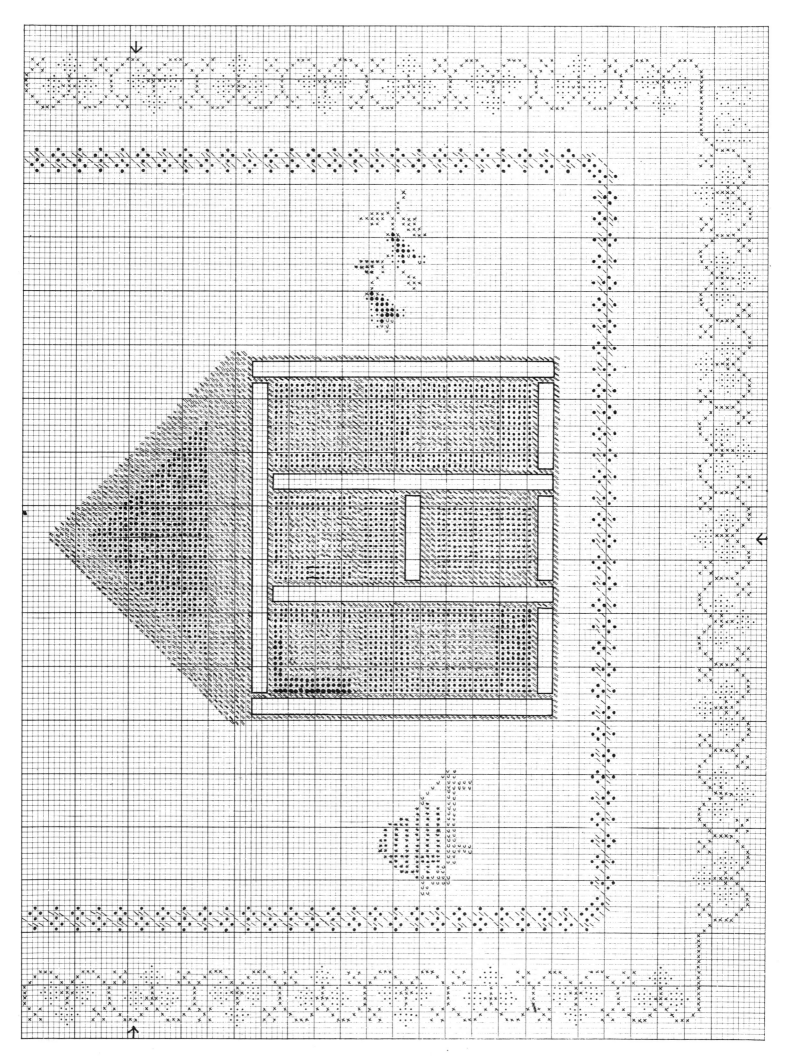

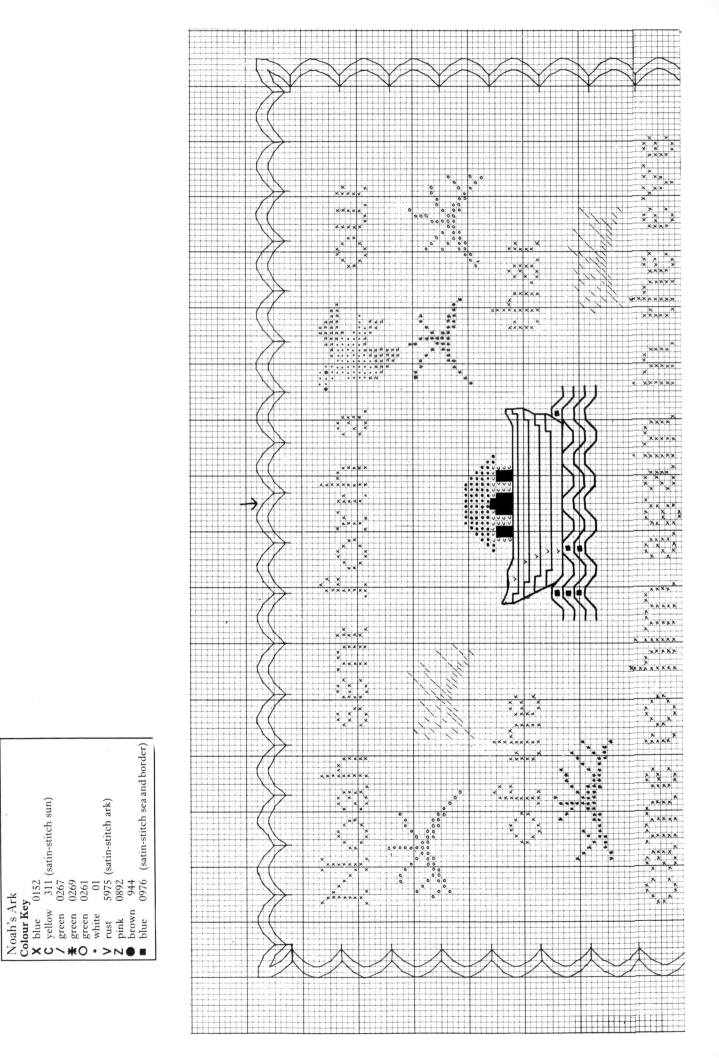

Noah's Ark
Colour Key
X	blue	0152	
C	yellow	311	(satin-stitch sun)
/	green	0267	
✳	green	0269	
O	green	0261	
•	white	01	
V	rust	5975	(satin-stitch ark)
Z	pink	0892	
●	brown	944	
■	blue	0976	(satin-stitch sea and border)

Deer motif (see p116)

Daisy motif (see p 116)

Blackwork Sampler

17

Blackwork Sampler

(colour photograph page 100, chart pages 114-15)

This is a collection of traditional sixteenth- and seventeenth-century blackwork motifs, symbols, borders and all-over repeat patterns, densely packed so as to include as many different designs as possible. The sampler can be worked as it is, or patterns or motifs used for your own design. It is intended as a reference piece. Black thread was traditional, but occasionally, paler more muted colours were used in shades of brown, green, blue and red. Later, blackwork designs were embellished with filling stitches and later still, richer fillings were used, incorporating metal threads, beads and seed pearls. 'Boxers' like the ones used in this sampler were filled with satin stitch, hence clothing them, perhaps out of modesty.

After working some designs in double running stitch you may be inspired to experiment with colours, filling stitches, beads and metal threads. Using stranded cottons will allow you to have different thicknesses of the thread to give plenty of variation in density and texture. This sampler includes the traditional 'boxers', a lion, various insects, birds, fish, a pineapple, flowers and a number of borders and repeat patterns.

Note: A close, evenweave fabric is essential for this technique, as is a blunt needle of the correct size. Too large a needle will distort the woven threads, too small a needle will pierce and damage the individual threads, which will then not lie neatly.

Fabric
White hardanger, twenty-two double threads to 1in (2.5cm). The finished sampler measures 12 × 18in (30 × 45.5cm). When buying your fabric, allow an extra 8in (20cm) on every side.

Thread
Coats Coton à Broder.

Stitches (see Chapter 5)
Double running stitch worked over two double threads, *or* back stitch worked over two double threads.
Deer and daisy motifs: cross stitch (cross symbol on chart), worked over one double thread, with satin stitch for heads of daisies.

Colour Key
black 0403 × 4 skeins (approx)

Alphabets and Numerals
Alphabet 5, Numerals 18.

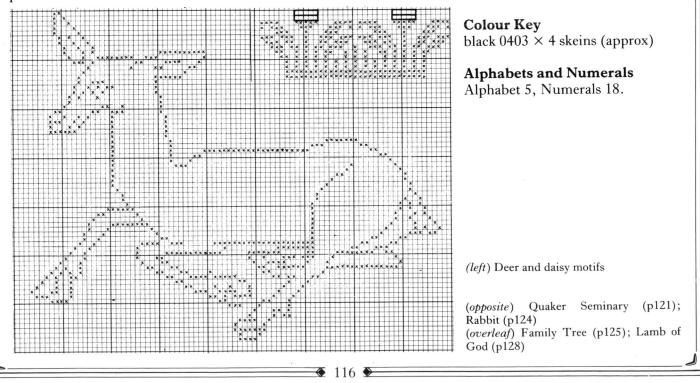

(left) Deer and daisy motifs

(opposite) Quaker Seminary (p121); Rabbit (p124)
(overleaf) Family Tree (p125); Lamb of God (p128)